BETRAYED

First published in Australia in 2009 by
New Holland Publishers (Australia) Pty Ltd
Sydney • Auckland • London • Cape Town

1/66 Gibbes Street, Chatswood NSW 2067 Australia
218 Lake Road Northcote Auckland 0746 New Zealand
86 Edgware Road London W2 2EA United Kingdom
80 McKenzie Street Cape Town 8001 South Africa

National Library of Australia Cataloguing in Publication data:
Ali, Latifa.
Betrayed / Latifa Ali with Richard Shears.
ISBN: 9781741108118 (pbk.)
Ali, Latifa.
Women--Iraq--Biography.
Women spies--Australia--Biography.
Iraq--Social conditions.
Iraq--Social life and customs.
Iraq War, 2003---Biography.

Other Authors/Contributors:
Shears, Richard.

305.4092

Publisher: Fiona Shultz
Publishing Manager: Lliane Clarke
Junior Editor: Ashlea Wallington
Proof-reader: Caroyln Beaumont
Designer: Natasha Hayles
Cover designer: Tania Gomes
Production manager: Olga Dementiev
Printer: KHL Printing Co Pte (Singapore)

10 9 8 7 6 5 4 3 2 1

Some names in this book have been changed for security reasons.

Betrayed

Escape from Iraq

Latifa Ali with Richard Shears

NEW
HOLLAND

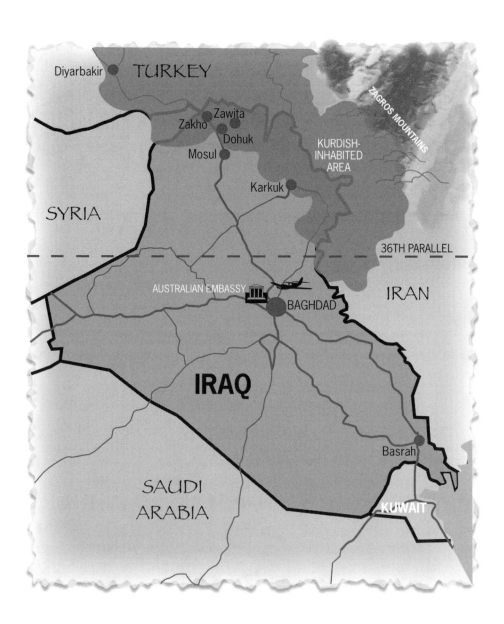

PROLOGUE

By now the first of the snows were beginning to fall across the Zagros Mountains and the track was treacherous—steep ravines fell away to the fast-flowing Great Zab River, feeding the plains of Kurdistan below. Soon the paths through the mountain range would be impassable and with the temperature plunging to minus 10°C the freedom fighters would return to their towns and villages, knowing that the Iraqi troops—and the Iranians who were always trying to penetrate the border—would be doing the same. But that would be several weeks away and none of the freedom fighters, the Peshmerga, were ready to leave just yet.

A blanket wrapped around his traditional dark-khaki uniform, the guerrilla continued his climb to where he knew Khalid had positioned himself. Then he broke away from the path and began scaling the steep sides. Khalid would already have seen him from his sniper's position but he felt quite safe, for no Arab soldier would travel alone through this territory unless he was pretending to be a Kurdish fighter and that would be a suicidal mission.

'Khalid,' he called against the icy wind, 'Khalid, I've brought the news you've been waiting for.'

The sniper burst up from his rocky cover. His checkered scarf hid his grin as he lifted his head high into the falling snowflakes and cried: 'Allah be praised!'

Then he turned to the messenger. 'A boy? A girl?'

'I don't know, Khalid. This is the only word they've sent. There's a car waiting to take you back.'

Khalid was 28 years old and very fit. He did not waste a moment. With his Kalashnikov thumping against his back on its strap he slithered down the hill, hit the path and ran on down towards the plains. Several times he slipped and came close to falling into the ravine, but his excitement overrode the danger. Then he tripped again, rolled and when he picked himself up he discovered he had lost his shoes. He looked around for them but realised they must have gone over the edge.

Now it was his bare feet which carried him over the stones. Tiny smears of his blood stained the light covering of snow, but he did not care about the pain. He wanted to reach his baby.

The 100 kilometre car journey seemed endless. He urged the driver on—'go faster, faster!'—through the villages and then the streets of Mosul before at last they reached his home.

His 16-year-old wife, Baian, with the baby in her arms, smiled as he burst into the bedroom, where other female members of the family were gathered.

She held the baby up. 'Here is your daughter,' she said.

'Ah, so I have a girl,' said Khalid. He didn't care that his first born was not a boy. There would be plenty of time for that.

'Your feet,' whispered one of the women. 'You are bleeding. Where are your shoes?'

'Somewhere up on the mountain,' he said dismissively. 'It doesn't matter.'

But it did. The loss of his shoes was to shape the destiny of the tiny baby girl he held so proudly in his arms on that cold November day in 1980.

ONE

I'm known as Latifa—'the gentle one'—now, although that's not the name my parents gave me. But dangers that came to surround me forced me to take on a new identity. Fear, threats and suffering—they are nothing new to me or my people, the Kurds, who for centuries have struggled to keep out invaders and have their independence recognised.

In the decades before I came into the world—and before Saddam Hussein began his own brutal oppression in the 1980s—the Kurdish people, who make up about 20 per cent of Iraq's 20 million population, had suffered persecution under Iraq's former leader, President Ahmad Hasan al-Bakr. By the time Saddam Hussein placed al-Bakr under house arrest and declared himself president in 1979, my father was a fierce and respected member of that honoured group of Kurdish freedom fighters, the Peshmerga.

And how he was needed. There had been fierce clashes between the Iraqi army and the guerrillas in 1977, but in the following two years hundreds of Kurdish villages were razed to the ground and more than 200,000 Kurds were deported to other parts of the country. I never found out how many soldiers my father killed up there in the mountains—I've seen him shoot and I know how good he is—and I know he would have been a one-man force to be reckoned with.

But now he was even more of a man among his peers. He was a father. And his bride, his wife, my mother, was among the most beautiful women in Iraq; blonde, green eyed and shapely, men would have killed for her hand but my father's family claimed her for him when she was just 15.

Baian was born in Dohuk, the name of which means 'small village', but with a population today of half a million it is anything but small. With the mountains and the Tigris River nearby, it is an attractive city and its university is recognised as one of the best in the region. But my mother's loveliness denied her any university education—in fact, her family were so concerned that she might be molested or raped by government agents who search towns and villages for attractive girls and women—that was the life—that they even kept her home from school. She became a prisoner of her beauty.

It was her father who gave Baian her education because he was a teacher and she had the added advantage of learning from her three brothers and four sisters when they came home from school. But while her early teenage years put her ahead of her peers as a scholar, she was never allowed to mix with girls of her own age.

My mother's and my father's families were distantly related through my great-great-grandmother, which was agreeable to everyone for it meant that when Baian and Khalid married the 'good genes' were passed on. The wedding, like all Kurdish ceremonies, was a grand affair, with singing and dancing and much merriment and then the couple retired to their room. This was where the bride would give herself to her husband and heaven forbid any woman who was found not to be a virgin. Just as in other households, his mother and his oldest brother waited outside Baian' and Khalid's bedroom door for the moment when Khalid emerged. Then they went in and, taking no notice of the bride, inspected the bed. They were looking for 'the blood on the cloth'. Yes, she was a true virgin and Khalid, well, he was now a man among men. Music was played, baklava was served. There was great rejoicing.

My father was to tell me years later, when I was old enough to understand, that he came to truly love my mother, although to this day I believe this is all the wrong way around and that love must come first. However, this was the Kurdish region of northern Iraq and that was the way things were.

Like his young bride, Khalid was well educated. He was born in Mosul, the regional capital, Iraq's fourth largest city and some 40 miles to the south of my mother's city of Dohuk, and shortly after leaving high school he worked hard at setting up his own welding business. All his employees were family members and the business flourished, so his bride and the family they would raise were guaranteed a good start to life.

As is the way, Khalid and Baian's marital home was his family's house, a three-storey building in the middle of the city. It was crowded, because they shared it with Khalid's parents, his seven sisters and a brother. And it was expected of the new bride that she would be a slave to the whole family, doing the cooking, washing and cleaning. She had moved from one domestic prison before her marriage to another as a new bride.

After three months Baian found herself pregnant with me. Again, it was a victory for Khalid. Now he was free to return to the mountains with the Peshmerga, for whom he had been fighting before his marriage, leaving his relatives to run the welding business. His wife was pregnant and while she coped with that he could fight for Kurdish independence until the time came when his baby was born. During those summer months he dressed himself in the traditional Peshmerga clothing of baggy harem pants and a khaftan top, while around his waist was a wide black belt in which he carried his ammunition and his dagger.

I learned from my mother how I was raised in my first few months. Like all children I was strapped very tightly into a cot so I wouldn't fall out as they rocked it back and forth. I've looked at family photos of my mother holding me and seen the smile on my father's face as he gazed at me. But there is one photo that I'll never forget. It shows me, still a baby, giggling at the camera my father is aiming at me— but my mother, who is holding me in her arms, is glaring at me. I've studied it so many times over the years and wondered whether, from those very early months of my life, Baian had seen me as a burden. I've tried to pass it off as a trick of the camera, one of those unguarded moments where an expression is not a true reflection of feelings, but I'm convinced now that the photo caught the truth.

There is no doubt that my mother suffered among her husband's sisters. Her beauty was outstanding and there would have been intense jealousy among her sisters-in-law. She put up with the ill-feeling, although she rebelled when the demands on her became too much.

'I've got a baby to care for,' she told the others. 'I can't wait hands and foot on you all as well.'

But Khalid insisted that she had to do what was asked of her. It was the way.

Baian gave birth to my brother when I was two. It seemed that despite her education and her fine looks she was destined to a life of domesticity, growing old, surrounded by children and ageing relatives. But dramatic events lay ahead that were to change all our lives in a way we could never have imagined.

Six months after my brother Bawar was born—in 1982—a close and trusted friend of my father who had connections with the Iraqi government gave him information that terrified him. Ten families had been singled out for execution by Saddam Hussein's troops, or agents. When caught, the families would be driven into the desert and shot. My family was among them.

'But how do they know about me?' asked Khalid 'I don't believe any of my people will have betrayed me.'

What he then learned devastated him. Inside one of his shoes which he had lost on the mountain more than two years earlier, was a piece of paper containing his name and his family's address. Most of the militia carried this single piece of identification with them so that if they were killed, their colleagues—who would not always know everyone's name—could inform their family of the death. The shoe with that incriminating piece of paper had apparently been found by Saddam's men. To my father's name they had added mine, my mother's, and my baby brother's.

There was now no choice. My parents had to flee Kurdistan. Those on Saddam's hit list contacted one another and escape routes were planned. It was suggested to my father that we should leave with a group of four other families—my father's relatives, meanwhile, would leave the family home and stay with cousins in other parts of Kurdistan. But as for travelling with four other families, he was against it.

'We'll go on our own,' he told the others. He refused to listen to warnings that there was safety in numbers.

We left under cover of darkness, driven by friends to the foot of the mountains and then I was loaded onto a donkey—I was but only two and have my parents' recollections of that journey. My father had always said that the mountains were the best friends of the Kurds, for they provided a barrier from any invaders and if you knew them, they were the best place to hide. And my father knew them well. We had to travel by night for safety but the hours of darkness were already bitterly cold, for it was autumn and the temperature was approaching zero.

My mother carried Bawar on her shoulders, following behind the donkey with me on its back and my father leading it from the front. Our destination was Iran, where my father had relatives in the capital, Tehran. Thankfully there was a reasonable telephone link between Mosul and Tehran and my father had been able to put a call through to say we were leaving Kurdistan. The journey through the mountains was expected to take 15 days and at the Iranian end we would have to bypass any Customs posts, for we had no passports. There were isolated villages that we reached in a kind of no-man's-land, where we were given food and shelter during the day and a chance to sleep. After all, these were people that, in his role as a militia my father had protected from pockets of marauding Iraqi troops. Sometimes, though, there were no places to stay and we had to rest in a tent and even caves. My father had prepared us well for the journey, but there was no telling how fate would play a part and almost bring about a disaster. We were about half way through the journey when the donkey lost its footing.

Luckily, I was strapped on or I would have been thrown into a ravine to my death. But the donkey was half over the edge, with its lead still in my father's hands, and it was only his incredible strength and fitness that was holding it back from a fatal plunge. But he couldn't pull the donkey back. Another few seconds and he wouldn't be able to hold on.

My mother reached over the squealing, terrified animal and

managed to pull me free. Now the donkey's lead was wrapped around my father's hand, the weight of the animal tightening the strap and making it impossible to free himself. They were both going to fall. But he was able to pull out his knife and sever the leash, saving himself but he could not prevent the poor donkey from falling to its death. Years later, Khalid was to tell me that there was no question what he would have done—if it came to it, he would have given his life to save me.

My parents continued that terrifying journey—for who knew who was watching us?—towards Iran. We passed through an area Khalid's relatives had revealed to us as being safe from border guards and, equally importantly, mines. We were picked up from the outskirts of a frontier village and driven to Tehran. We were safe. But within days my father was breaking down in tears. In a phone call to friends in Mosul he learned that the other families we were asked to travel with had all been caught making their escape and had been executed. His tears were of sadness for them and relief for us all because his instincts—and his knowledge of the mountains—had saved his family.

We could not return to Kurdistan for the foreseeable future. We were refugees. As my parents settled me and my brother in with my father's relatives they discussed our future. It seemed that Iran, now at war with Iraq, was not prepared to accept us. Years later, in the mid 1980s, Iran was to give its support to the Peshmerga, but in the meantime my parents decided to keep a low profile as far as the authorities were concerned. Through human rights groups they discovered their options. We might be able to find a new home in several countries that had shown a willingness to accept refugees from Kurdistan, including some of the Scandinavian nations and Poland. We had many relatives in Sweden—no less than 16 families, all related in one way or another—and that was my parents' choice. But it was not to be. Arrangements were made for us to be transferred to Poland and from there we could seek an onward destination.

My parents haven't told me much about our sojourn in Poland except to tell me that we were in limbo there for more than a year. By now my father had a passport, with his wife, my brother and I sharing the identity page. Applications were made to settle in several Western countries; then the Australians offered us a home as migrants. By now it was 1983 and Kurdistan was in turmoil. It was in that year that the Kurdish Democratic Party, led by Massoud Barzani, was at the forefront of an Iranian thrust into northern Iraq and many people were being killed or displaced. As if the Kurds had not suffered enough through the earlier clashes with the Iraqi army and the Peshmerga, when tens of thousands of people were forced into other parts of the country. Terrible reports were reaching the West of genocide being carried out by Saddam Hussein's troops, who were also engaged in the war with Iran. Not only are the Kurds ethnically closer to the Iranians, the main reason for Saddam's hatred for the people of the north was the fact that the Kurds were fighting side by side with Iran's Revolutionary Guard against the Iraqi leader's forces.

In addition, there was the ongoing conflict between Kurdish rebels in neighbouring Turkey and that country's army, as the push for self rule by the Kurds across that whole region intensified. To add to the confusion, thousands of Turkish Kurd refugees poured across the border into Kurdistan. Who knows what the fate of my family would have been had we not fled, even if we had been able to avoid the execution warrant that had been issued against us.

My family was among the first wave of Kurdish refugees to be accepted by Australia and it was thanks to my father's skills in engineering that we were given the privilege. What followed was the arrival of many thousands of Kurds, who were settled into the western suburbs of Sydney and the northern areas of Melbourne. By the time all the arrangements had been made, the interviews with officials concluded, paperwork completed, I was five years old when we arrived in Australia. I look at photographs these days and see how my father in particular would spoil me with toys. There I am sitting on a rug surrounded by dolls and other playthings, both in Poland and after our arrival in Australia. He doted over me.

Unlike refugees who jump the queue and end up in detention camps, we were provided with an apartment in the western suburb of Liverpool. My father had already had a job lined up, as a consultant and engineer at a welding factory. Other Kurds were moving into the region and a small community began to build up. In time, we moved to another apartment, which was in a quieter area and where we had access to a swimming pool. My parents could already speak English—don't forget, my mother had a brilliant education from her father, a teacher, and my own father was well educated, too—and when we were at home they spoke in both Kurdish and English. So my early childhood was privileged in that I learned both languages.

I was enrolled in the Liverpool junior public school, where there were a mixture of children from other countries—Chinese, Italians, Greeks, Lebanese. I was the only Iraqi girl, and other students, not even having heard of Kurdistan, thought that I was Italian. One day, when a Lebanese girl asked where I was from and I told her she said: 'Oh, you're one of us, then.' But I had come from a proud Kurdish family and I quickly pointed out to her that the Kurds are like no others in that region—we were ethnically different and had our own language and dialects.

My mother was adamant that we should cling to our heritage.

'Do not mix with Arabs when you meet them,' she would tell me time and again. 'While we are from northern Iraq, we are different. Always remember that. I don't want you to be fanatical about it, but always remember who you are, where you are from.'

While my mother had implored me not to be fanatical, she was obsessed with doing whatever she could to help the Kurds, both in Australia and in Iraq. She started working for a Kurdish radio station, reading the news in three different dialects and also writing her own poetry and reading that out, too. People would say to me: 'Your mother is very talented—she's a news reader and an entertainer all rolled into one.'

She was also a woman of contrasts as far as the Kurds were concerned. While she went out of her way to help newcomers settle in and give advice over the radio—even taking people to hospital by taxi if the need arose and asking nothing in return—she didn't like us mingling with the Kurdish community in general, unless it was for special events, such as newroz—New Year's Day—but which marks the time in 612 BC that the Kurds' existence was first recognised when the ancestors of today's Kurdish people rose up against the Assyrian empire.

Baian was still a very beautiful woman but as often happens, her blonde hair had now darkened and taken on a reddish sheen. But she turned men's heads wherever she went. Even in my younger years I could see how they were attracted to her. And I could see how, as the months rolled by, my parents began to see less and less of each other. While she ran back and forth from the house, caring for us children when we were home from school and going to the radio station, my father was always absent except for late in the evening. His job as both a worker and a consultant was very demanding and it was only at weekends that we were able to be united as a family. We might go to the beach at Cronulla or sit on the banks of the George's River for a picnic.

While these were peaceful scenes, my parents were distressed at the news that was pouring out of Kurdistan—news that my mother in her role at the radio station was among the first to hear. In mid-March 1988, Saddam Hussein unleashed his most evil weapon of mass destruction against the Kurds, using poison gas on the town of Halabja, killing up to 5000 people and leaving thousands more to die of terrible complications, such as disease and birth defects for years afterwards. Human Rights Watch declared the attack as an act of genocide and to this day it is the biggest chemical weapons attack against any civilian-populated area. My parents were devastated—but remained thankful that their relatives were out of reach of the gas clouds.

It was when I began my senior education at Liverpool Girls High School that my mother implored my father to find us a new home. There were, she complained, too many Middle Eastern people moving into the district. Looking back on that time I can see that it was a strange kind of racism but because I was still young I didn't see anything wrong in her comments. In any case, we moved to an apartment in nearby Chipping Norton, which my father was able to purchase on a mortgage because his wages from the factory were very good.

Among the girls I befriended at high school was another Kurd—her family knew mine. As she was a newcomer my mother asked me to look after her, guide her around, show her where she could buy nice clothes. My mother even helped the family financially and told me that I should remember to do the same thing for other Kurds if they needed help. It was curious that while she did not want to mix with them, she went out of her way to help them, like a shadowy benefactor. I've come to realise, though—oh, how I have realised—that her reluctance to keep her distance was due to the idle gossip that began as soon as her back was turned. She had had enough of it in Iraq, the unceasing chatter about this family and that, how much they earned, what kind of furniture they had, how they got on with their children or this cousin or that aunty.

In any case, I did as my mother asked and helped the new girl, Sheireen, who was among a group of some 50 families who had arrived in Australia in 1992 following more uprisings in the north and south of Iraq in the wake of the Gulf War. I told Sheireen that if anyone bullied her, if she needed any help whatsoever, she could come to me. I introduced her to teachers, to my school friends, helped her buy the best learning books, to say no to drugs, who to avoid. Although she could speak English—she had picked it up in a refugee camp before arriving in Australia—she was still in great need of guidance and I was there for her. How it hurts me now to think of the betrayal that was to come. By her and so many others.

Two

My schoolgirl days were fun—and rebellious. I skipped classes to go to the movies or the swimming pool and gossiped with my classmates about the boys in the school next door. We unashamedly talked about our crushes. There was a pool in our apartment complex which also had adjoining tennis courts. The first thing each morning, before heading off to school, I would jump in the pool and do a few laps, along with my brother. I was good at sports, doing karate training at weekends, a skill my parents had insisted on me taking up, and getting picked in the school team at netball. I had also been playing the piano—classical music—since I was eight. Sometimes I'd rollerskate around a nearby lake, racing my brother on his skateboard. It was great fun. We were real Aussie kids!

My parents—although Muslims, they were not strong adherents to the faith—had given me the freedom to do pretty much what I wanted, except that they made sure I stayed in at night in my early teens, telling me I was still too young, even though many of my classmates were out and about after dark. My father was what you would call a worldly man, enjoying his vodka and his cigarettes, and telling my brother that when the time came he would rather he drank and smoked in front of him than behind his back. He was happy to let me wear a bikini when I went to the swimming pool. And neither of my parents objected to me drawing naked pictures of women, supporting my art and asking me what I was trying to convey.

But when it came to boys, they were very protective of me. I was allowed to go to school discos on weekends as long as it was with a group of girls, who my father would pick up and take, and then he would make sure to come back for me later. My parents told me nothing about the whys and wherefores of sex—it was left to my school teacher to explain those things to the class of girls, holding up a cucumber and fitting a condom over it, saying that this was how you avoided getting nasty diseases or falling pregnant.

The time came when I found myself a boyfriend, an Anglo-Australian. Of all places to meet, it was in the library, which was shared by both the girls' and boys' schools. Realising my parents would frown on me, still in my early teens, 'seeing a boy' meant we had to meet in secret. Patrick, a good sportsman himself, had an old car and whenever the chance arose, he would drive us to Parramatta or some big centre where my mother was unlikely to be during her rounds of the Kurdish community. We'd flirt with one another in McDonald's and hold hands at afternoon picture matinees, but it never went any further than that.

During school holidays, our parents took us on no less than four trips to Germany, where we had a number of relatives. When I say 'a number' I mean no less than 300! I enjoyed the trips there, meeting new cousins who seemed to be just about everywhere, yet each time as we flew home to Australia, I felt a sense of excitement. Australia had really grown on me and it was, after all, where my friends were.

My mother had a powerful influence on all around her, to the point that many women in the community resented her. Perhaps it was because she was sharper than them, or it may have had something to do with the way their husbands would stare admiringly at her and hover around her at Kurdish events she might attend. They would find any excuse to talk to her about politics, history, anything that would engage her in conversation. I would later hear comments, passed on by my friends, about what a mismatch my parents seemed to be. My mother was slim and beautiful with high cheekbones and my father was a short, dark, Arab-looking man with a beard.

Her beauty opened many doors for her within the Kurdish community in Australia and also when she was on visits to Kurdistan. In my younger days, I never knew what she did on those trips but I came to learn later that in 1992, when I was 12 and she was abroad she had been arrested in Turkey, pretending to be a Turkish refugee in one of the border camps. She had been caught taking photographs to gain evidence of how the Turks were treating the Kurds and she was thrown into prison. It took a begging phone call from a high official in the Kurdish resistance of Massoud Barzani, to the Turks to win her freedom. At home in Sydney she was a wife, a mother and a newsreader at a radio station. Overseas, God knew what role she played.

In 1994, as I was approaching my 14th birthday, my mother had a surprise for me. She was pregnant. She gave birth to my sister a whole 13 years after her last child—my brother—and she was still only 30. Curiously, I felt that the arrival of baby Bojeen did nothing to lessen the sense of restlessness that I was beginning to see in my mother. She had already thrown herself into the community, was out and about everywhere, and now this little baby had come along. But she still gave me the impression that she wanted to continue to, well, 'explore' is the best way I can put it. Now she had a baby to look after, as well as continuing to do our cooking, tending to household needs and maintaining her work at the radio station. And she continued to help Kurds financially, not only in Australia but by sending money overseas to them. It was my father's money that he had earned, yet he did not object as long as her generosity was not going to disadvantage his own family. In any case, he trusted her implicitly, handling as she did all our cheque books and being in charge of the bank statements.

Somehow, my mother still managed to fit in the time to help people locally. Shortly after my sister was born, a new Kurdish family arrived in Liverpool and the daughter, who was 18, wanted to stop wearing the *hijab*, the Muslim scarf. She felt out of place at school among other girls with their hair flowing freely. One evening, when we went to visit the family, my mother spoke to the parents in general terms about how girls in Australia had a right to 'be themselves'. She even revealed her knowledge of the Koran by reciting how no-one should be forced to do anything because that would be against God's will. The very next day, the girl turned up at school without the scarf. It was an example of my mother's influence.

When did I realise that things were going wrong between my parents? Perhaps it was when I was just 12 or 13, when I recall my mother telling me how she had been a victim of a forced—she didn't use the word 'arranged'—marriage at the age of just 15. And I remember comments like 'I wish I'd never married your father'. They would never argue in front of me, but I heard her say to him once that it was all his fault that we had had to flee from

Kurdistan—obviously a reference to the time he had lost his shoe with that incriminating information tucked inside.

Sometimes, after I heard them in animated discussions in the bedroom, my mother would storm out of the house and not return for several hours. And there was the time when I came home and saw a couple of champagne glasses on the table.

'Oh, who came by?' I asked my mother, surprised to see drink glasses there in the middle of the afternoon.

'None of your business,' she replied.

And then there was the lingerie. She was shopping around for really sexy, expensive, designer label underwear and it certainly wasn't the kind of thing my father would have been interested in. So who was she trying to impress? I never saw my mother with another man, but then, my parents had never seen me with my boyfriend from the library. There was always a way.

If my father ever came home from work early enough, before we, the children, went to bed, we would have a family chat about work and school. I was always groaning about maths, while my brother was proudly talking about his achievements in that subject. Soon a new topic began to creep into the conversations, very insidiously at first but, in time I realised it was all part of a master plan my mother had hatched.

'Those holidays we've had in Germany—you children enjoyed them, didn't you.' It was a statement rather than a question.

'Oh yeah,' my brother and I replied, thinking that another vacation to Europe was in her mind.

While she left it there the first time she raised the topic, Germany began to enter the conversations more frequently until finally when we had once again said how much we had enjoyed our holidays there, she turned to my father in front of us and said: 'There you are, I told you they'd enjoy living there. It's a far better life and we'd be much closer to our relatives in Iraq than here in Australia.'

Suddenly I realised what she was proposing. 'Wait!' I cried. 'What are you saying? That you want us all to leave and live in Germany?'

'That's what I'm saying. Your father and I have discussed it.'

'But I've got all my friends here! There's my education—I want to do my Higher School Certificate and start a career. You know that I may want to be a doctor or perhaps be a forensic analyst, something like that. And you've always told me that knowledge is power.'

Baian had all the answers, of course.

'You can finish your Higher School Certificate in Germany. It will be better for your resumé to show that you completed your education over there.'

I was 17 at the time and I had to concede to my mother's argument. Life wouldn't be so bad in Germany and being there would not harm my academic progress. I felt sorry for my father, though. He had agreed to stay behind to put all our affairs in order, including selling the house. As soon as he had sold it, he would send the money on to an account my mother was going to set up in Germany and then come over to join us.

'It will be money for you, for your futures,' he told my brother and me. 'And of course your little sister will benefit from it too, in time.'

But there was something I had found out about our finances that my father was not aware of. One day, in my mother's absence, curiosity led me to look at the bank statements. I was surprised to see that some $200,000—money that my father had earned through all those long hours he was working—had been withdrawn. I was to find out in time that it had been sent to my uncles—my mother's brothers—in Kurdistan for a sinister reason that I would later learn about. How I wish I'd had the foresight to understand what the future held as my mother made preparations for us to fly to Germany.

My father came to the airport to see us off. It was the summer of 1998. My father hugged me and kissed me on the cheek.

'Don't say goodbye, Dad,' I said. 'We'll be seeing you when you come to join us.'

We flew to Dusseldorf and then travelled to the university city of Siegen, in the west of Germany, some 50 miles east of Cologne. The pursuit of knowledge in that city had taken over from the iron ore mining industry of old. I was soon to learn why the town was popular with Kurdish people—with its white buildings set against a background of mountains, it would have reminded many of northern Iraq, eastern Turkey and the Zagros Ranges. Its one big claim to fame is that the painter Rubens was born there. On the way I had asked my mother who we knew there. She told me we had a very nice relative, a distant cousin, who had lived there since he was a teenager, was now a prominent lawyer and also owned a pizza restaurant.

We stayed at first in a small apartment owned by one of our relatives in the centre of the city and it wasn't long before I was introduced to the distant cousin. My mother had been invited to a Kurdish party and, with the baby being cared for, my brother and I went along with her.

'There's someone here I'd like you to meet,' she said and led us to a tall, handsome man who immediately reminded me of the Welsh singer, Tom Jones. I thought he was 'cool'. He spoke English, which was a relief because everyone else around us seemed to be speaking in Kurdish or German. We had, my mother informed me, met 'him' before on one of our holidays to Germany but I had been too young to remember him.

After a few weeks my mother found us a place to live in the mediaeval city of Munster, directly to the north of Siegen. I asked my mother who we knew there. She told me that was where this distant cousin lived. Our new place was a townhouse apartment, very art deco with a wooden floor and three bedrooms, my mother and baby sister in one bedroom and my brother and I having one room each. The place was too dark and heavy for my liking, but perhaps I was unfairly comparing it with our bright home in Australia.

It was in that city that my mother's friend had his legal practice and a pizza restaurant, and where my mother arranged for me to take German lessons at a foreign language school. Munster is known as the bicycle capital of Germany but it was also home to a large British forces base. In between my language lessons, my mother lined me up to work as a waitress at his restaurant. I answered the phone and served the pizzas—mainly to British servicemen who filled the place out. I got on well with them. They were always making cheeky 'come on' remarks, but always in a jokey way. I realised why he wanted me there—I was pulling in the British customers because they could chat to me in English.

Despite my mother's assurances that I could finish my HSC on leaving Australia, it turned out to be impossible because the tests were all in German—and I still had a long way to go before I was proficient enough to understand even the spoken language. I loved the people in the city and so did my brother, who was attending high school while also learning German. He was now of an age when the girls were giving him the eye. His ambition was to go on to college to study electrical engineering and he was to prove himself a brilliant scholar with languages, picking up Arabic, Persian and German.

I felt under a great deal of pressure from my mother, who obviously didn't want to see me fail at anything I chose to do. She had overcome many obstacles in her life, given that she had been married off so young, and she was determined that her daughter would do well, too. In time my brother started working at the pizza restaurant as a delivery 'boy' and, being so personable, he made a lot of tips.

My brother and I were very close—we had been since we were youngsters and many people had thought when we were young children that we were twins. How well I remember that first day in Australia when I started primary school and he was going into the adjoining kindergarten. With our mother, we turned up hand in hand and this was to be the first time that he and I would be separated. When the teachers came and started to lead us away in different directions he was so frightened at being taken away from me that he bawled his head off and peed his pants.

Bawar was not only my younger brother—he grew up to be my best friend and we would share our silly secrets. He knew about my school boyfriend, the boy from the library, and he would back me up in protecting my flirting. If I was on the phone to Patrick, Bawar might call: 'Hang up quick, Mum's coming!' Yes, that was my brother and now we were far away from Sydney, still together, still close.

It was while I was enjoying my first months in Munster that Bawar and I joined up with his friends from school and we went along to a nightclub. I'd been to discotheques in Australia but this was something quite different. The air was full of a sweet, smokey smell, which I quickly learned was marijuana. I was not tempted to try it, but I did have a sip of vodka, just to experience what my father enjoyed and almost spit it out. 'How can anybody drink this stuff?' I cried. I couldn't understand how my father could enjoy it so much during his nightly ritual, pouring a glass of the liquor to take with his plate of babaganou and homous.

My brother and I still retained a great respect for our mother—despite the sternness that she sometimes displayed and my earlier suspicions about someone she might have been seeing in Australia—so when she gave us a key to let ourselves in whenever we went out to a nightclub we did not take advantage of the freedom she afforded us. We always made sure we got home at a reasonable time—certainly no later than 2am, which we believed was reasonable for nightclubbers!

In time, as the months rolled by and my German lessons progressed, our cousin asked if I felt confident enough to convert some English documents into German, and vice versa. At first, as I sat in his legal office, I was hesitant, but my confidence grew as my lessons continued. Working in this way improved my German more and he seemed very happy with my work. In between my jobs for our cousin, sometimes at the pizza restaurant, sometimes in his office, I also found employment at a clothing boutique selling designer clothes from all around Europe. I was trying to earn as much as possible so I could buy a return ticket to Australia to visit my father. There was yet another little business I became involved with—my very own! Once a month an international festival was held at which I had a small stall and sold my own jewellery. Our cousin had helped me by finding where I could obtain the beads from Spain, Morocco and other parts of the African continent.

But as for my father. . . where was he? Even though I was saving up money for the fare to visit him, I wondered why he hadn't come to Germany yet. It was a question I was starting to ask my mother. She told me to be patient because some things moved slowly—just what was she up to? She had started travelling back and forth to London, taking my young sister, now five, with her. Sometimes when I answered the phone, men with heavily accented Arab voices would ask in English if my mother was there. When I asked who was calling, I was given names that I later established were well known in the Kurdish government. It became quite obvious that my mother was involved politically with them in some way. It is a fact that in time she was operating as a broker to send agricultural machinery from Germany to Kurdistan but I believed from the snatches of conversation I heard as she spoke on the phone that her work was not simply that of a broker. Government officials were named in her conversations and there was never any reference to machinery or costs. Whatever those political conversations were about, I never really heard enough to form any strong conclusions.

One day I asked her outright: 'Mum, when you fly to London, what do you do?'

She turned on me, surprised that I should have asked such a question. 'You're too young for any of this,' she snapped. 'Just keep on doing what you're doing, improve more so you can go to university.'

I told her that I could do so much better if I was home in Australia. I missed Sydney so much. My brother, too, who had had so many friends at high school, was feeling just as homesick for Australia. He used to love cricket and I'd hear him asking at our new home, 'Isn't there any TV channel anywhere in the whole of Germany that has the cricket?'

But there was relief at times from the dreariness of life in Germany; our mother would take us on a holiday to other European countries such as Italy, Switzerland and Spain for a couple of weeks. We would almost always go by train and we really lorded it because my mother was earning good money from—well, from whatever work she was doing for the Kurdish government. We stayed in the best hotels, ate fine foods and enjoyed the sunshine. It was bliss while it lasted but of course we always had to return to Germany to that big, dark apartment of ours.

I had also met a friend of my brother's, Ojo, who was half German, half African. He was good fun to be with and the three of us would often head off to a coffee shop—where I would drink tea—or go to the cinema together, particularly as it helped me with the language. Sometimes I met Ojo on his own and we'd chat about everything under the sun. I had to be careful, however, that my mother did not see him with me. I was very much aware that she did not approve of black people, even those who were of mixed race, perhaps because of her own Aryan descendancy, revealed in her lovely green eyes and the lighter-coloured hair that she had had in her younger days.

But I still felt a great loneliness, eminating, I suspected from a desire to return to Australia. Germany felt so crowded compared to Australia and the sky seemed to bear down on me as if it was lower. It was a relief when our mother would take us to Siegen to visit our cousins and it was one of these trips, when I was 18 that I met my cousin Mikael, who was four years older than me. In fact, I'd been introduced to him before, when I was 12, and I'd thought he was fun. I had also met up with him when my family took us to Kurdistan in my early teens and he was also on a visit there. Now he was 23 years old and, I thought, very handsome—tall, dark with a cheeky grin. Having been raised in Germany, he was very Westernised, but his parents still retained their strong cultural traditions. He was still at university, studying international law, but I was soon to find out that he had a frightening dark side.

'You know he's very interested in you,' one of my female cousins whispered to me during our latest trip to Siegen.

'Oh nonsense,' I said. 'You won't find me going out with him'— but secretly I would have loved to have gone on a date with him.

As things turned out we agreed when we got chatting at a relative's wedding to meet up for a coffee. In time, our short coffee sessions developed into brunch, then lunch and walks in the park. Although I'd had a few crushes on boys in Sydney, and had a platonic boyfriend from the school library, I felt something much stronger with Mikael. I was falling for him but I certainly didn't want my mother to find out. I always felt that she was hovering close by, even though she wasn't, of course.

Because we were travelling back and forth to Siegen quite

frequently I took every opportunity to meet Mikael. During our rendezvous in parks and coffee shops, he gradually told me about his 'after dark' activities. He revealed them so gradually to me that I wasn't shocked. Just a little hint here, a small suggestion there, but taken as a whole, what he was doing was frightening. He and a group of other cousins, along with associates from the Turkish, Arabic and Moroccan community were breaking into shops and homes and stockpiling their stolen goods in a warehouse. One day in a coffee shop, Mikael pulled back his jacket and showed me the butt of a handgun.

'My God, where did you get that?' I asked.

'Oh, I've got plenty more where these come from,' he said. ' I can get hash, pills, anything.'

'No thank you,' I said harshly.

While I was falling for him, I was also deeply disturbed about his revelations. I know I should have walked away from him—but my feelings for him had become so strong that each time I told myself to stay away I found myself being drawn back. So I found out more. His parents, he said, accepted that he could 'acquire' anything that they might want, although he never revealed any of the stuff was stolen. Once, he told me, he took home a container of live, deadly snakes that he planned to sell to a collector, but in the meantime they were being kept in the bath at his home.

'But they'll get out and bite someone!' I exclaimed.

'They can't get out of the bath. . . too slippery,' he assured me.

I ventured to raise the subject of Mikael's activities with a cousin and she said she knew he was 'up to no good' and suggested we should follow him one night 'to see what these boys are up to'.

We followed him and a group of his friends on foot through the dark streets of Siegen, ducking behind cars or into shop doorways if they slowed down. Eventually they reached a park, where, before they slipped into total darkness I was able to make out who they were meeting—a group of men with Mohawk hairstyles, the symbol in those days of neo-Nazis.

'Let's get out of here,' my terrified cousin implored. 'If they spot us, we'll be raped and have our throats cut.'

But Mikael was so kind and gentle with me. He never said a harsh word to me. He treated me like a lady and, being just 18, I felt on top of the world whenever I was with him. Yet I never considered us as being in a relationship—for a start, I lived in Munster and he lived miles away in Siegen and we were only able to meet for two or three days every couple of months or so. And that was how it continued as the months rolled by, with me continuing my work with our cousin at his lawyer's office in between those visits from time to time to Siegen. Then, towards the end of 1999, as I approached my 19th birthday, we travelled south as usual, this time for a cousin's wedding. My mother told me we would be staying for three weeks. We were heading into a period when my life was to change for the worse.

When the time came, I just didn't feel like going to the wedding and I decided to remain at home. I'd heard that at Kurdish weddings in Germany, everybody looks at everybody else and the ceremony becomes the centre of gossip. Later that afternoon, as I sat alone reading, the phone rang. It was Mikael.

'Aren't you supposed to be at the wedding?' I asked.

'Yes, I'm supposed to be—but I'm not feeling too well. And you know what, Latifa? I have a longing for that delicious chicken and and sweet corn soup that I remember you making for us some time ago. You don't feel like making some for me, do you? I'm sure it will be the best medicine.'

I didn't see anything suspicious in the fact that this unwell man should be able to drive over to the flat to pick me up and take me back to his place, a two-storey house on the outskirts of town. He was dressed neatly in casuals and I could smell aftershave. I didn't think anything of it when he put on some music in the lounge room and started jiving around while I was in the kitchen making the soup.

Later, after we had finished eating, he suggested we watch a bit of TV. The TV was upstairs in his bedroom. I told him I could only stay for a short time because his aunt would be back from the wedding soon.

'Oh, they won't be back until midnight,' he laughed. 'Come on, let's go and watch some TV.'

I followed him up the stairs.

THREE

There was only one place to sit—or lie, as it turned out—and that was his single bed. He put the TV on, some German movie with the sound down low, and we lay propped up against the pillows. The only light was from a bedside lamp and the screen. We were so close that, inevitably, we started cuddling one another. I didn't mind—I really did like him and he wasn't a close cousin in any case.

'This is nice,' he said as he caressed my neck, 'but you know something? I'd really like to feel what you're really like. Really feel your skin up against mine. Can you understand that, Latifa?'

Yes, I understood. I felt the same way. Were they warning bells I could hear ringing somewhere in my mind? If they were, I ignored them as I slipped off my clothing.

I turned to Mikael. 'I want you to promise that this is as far as we go. I don't want to get pregnant. We can touch, we can enjoy the feeling of each other but that is all.'

'I swear to you,' he said, embracing me.

My thoughts raced back to school. To those ridiculous sex lessons. Don't have sex unless the man is protected. No matter what, don't let it happen. I began to have second thoughts as I felt him move around to lie on top of me. Suddenly there was a hand over my mouth; his legs were working against mine, I wanted to cry out, to shout 'No, stop! Stop!' But his hand was tight over my lips, I was struggling, pushing fighting—and then I felt a sharp stab of pain.

Moments later he rolled away from me, his hand falling from my face. My breath came in spasms. He'd had sex with me—that much I knew. Another flashback to those classroom lessons—pregnancy, disease. Oh dear God, what had happened? Had I been raped? Was it my fault? Had I led him on? Was that what sex was always like? So painful, so quick? So violent?

Thoughts raced through my mind as I felt him roll from the bed and then, with his bare back to me, I saw him look down at himself, before he reached for a towel on a chair

Then Mikael turned and grinned at me. But there was no warmth in his eyes. And even as the grin fell away to a stark, hard face, he said: 'Now you are mine. You are mine forever.'

I saw the towel. A glimpse of red.

'Now I love you even more,' he said. 'You cannot belong to anyone but me,' he said. 'No-one will want you.'

Panic raced through me. What was he talking about?

'We can now make arrangements for our marriage. You will not be able to refuse me.'

'Marriage?' I asked. I could hear the shock in my voice. 'What are you talking about?'

'It's simple. You're mine now.'

I asked him to take me home. We rode in silence, my hands

trembling, but as we passed under street lights—for by now darkness had descended—I could see the smile had returned to his face. My body was tense. Pain still ran through me. I felt like nails had been hammered into my body. I had a sudden impression of a painting by a Mexican artist, Frida Kahlo, who portrayed personal suffering in her works.

The following day I met a female cousin in a coffee shop. I was just curious, I told her, but what does it mean when a girl bleeds after having sex for the first time?

'Don't you know?' she asked, incredulously. Then she said: 'It means she's lost her virginity, of course. She's not pure any more in the eyes of other men or God.'

I felt so stupid. Naïve. I was angry with myself. What had I done? Mikael's voice came back to me. 'No-one will want you. You are mine forever.'

I wanted to find him and strangle him for using me, for taking something precious from me that could never be replaced. A precious part of my body. My honour.

Virginity and its loss had never been explained to me, neither in school nor at home. Up until now, I had not understood how precious it was.

I had to pretend to the cousin that I was following up on some gossip I'd heard about another girl. 'What do you mean she's not pure?' I asked.

'Well, it means that only the man who has taken away her virginity can claim her as his because no Muslim man will want to marry a woman who isn't a virgin—who has had sex before him. She has to marry the man who has taken her or she will be outcast as a slut.'

My heart sank. 'You must have heard of honour killings,' she continued. 'In Kurdistan, if your new husband or your family finds out you're not a virgin, they'll kill you. She'd be a disgrace to the family and her husband would be humiliated. Loads of women over there have been killed.'

I tried not to appear shocked.

I tried to control a shudder. Thank heavens I had grown up in the West. An Aussie girl. Free from such horrors. Thank God I was living in Germany where nobody seemed to care about such things. Sex was all over the TV, the cinemas, the billboards. Yet I felt so much shame. I felt betrayed by Mikael. He knew what he had done, what it meant for me. Of course, I would in time be free to marry anyone I eventually fell in love with, but his actions had denied me the chance of ever marrying anyone from my birth country, Kurdistan, and also from a just about every Muslim country in the world.

When I next saw Mikael at a family gathering, he whispered to me that he had to see me again. Never, I told him. Not after what he had done.

'But you won't have to be concerned like you were before,' he said. 'I'll wear a condom. There won't be any risk.'

He began ringing our apartment in Münster every day I was in that city. He'd call, too, at our cousin's legal office.

'Latifa, I'm going to marry you, you know,' he said.

'No, no, no. I'm too young to even think about marriage, I have my lessons to finish and I'm going to go home to Australia to be with my father soon, because he hasn't been able to get away yet to join us.'

'You can't do that,' said Mikael.

'I can do anything I like,' I retorted.

I'd had a chance to go back over that evening. I was now convinced that even though we had lain naked together, he had raped me. I had cried out for him to stop and he had smothered my voice and gone ahead. I wondered whether I should report him to the authorities, but the more I thought about it, the more I realised I was in a hopeless position. I had willingly undressed for a start—and did I really believe that the community would turn against one of their sons, who had grown up as a 'good Kurdish boy' among them? No, I was in a losing position from the start.

As the weeks went by, Mikael kept up the pressure. We hadn't even touched each other since that night but once it had happened, it seemed romance had vanished, for both him and me. I was already his, as far as he was concerned.

'I'm going to send my mother around to your house to ask for your hand.'

I thought that was a ridiculous thing to say, but I learned later that this was indeed the Kurdish way. Any man wanting to propose to a woman always did it through his mother. It would be the mother who would literally call around at a young woman's house and speak to her family. Rejection by either the family or the would-be bride was a great humiliation for the mother who knocked.

'Don't do that, Mikael,' I begged him. 'I don't want to marry you.'

But my mother liked him. He was handsome, he came from a good family—but she didn't know about his dark side; his drug dealing, weapons trading and finally the biggest sin of all, stealing my virginity. Yes, I had no doubt that it had been stolen from me in a brief moment in time and now I was a 'marked' woman for the rest of my life. If I found a husband for myself, a Western man, the loss of my virginity would probably not matter—but Mikael was going to send his mother to my home and my own mother would almost certainly agree to my betrothal. Knowing the deep affection my mother held for her Kurdish background, she would insist on my accepting Mikael's hand. If I refused, she would want to know why and I knew I would be too ashamed to tell her.

Did I lack courage at that time? It was more a sense of feeling utterly trapped. Still a teenager, I was living in a modern Western world yet I'd become ensnared in an ancient culture. Apart from the banter with the British soldiers in the pizza cafe, I realised that everyone around me was a Kurd. All my friends were Kurds. If we travelled south from Munster to Siegen it was to visit our Kurdish relatives. My mother was working for high people in Kurdistan, of that I had no doubt, although she never spelled it out to me. People who rang spoke Kurdish.

And so the day came when my mother approached me and said that Mikael wanted to marry me and she was very happy about it— and what did I think about it? I knew the pressure would continue if I said no. So, against all my instincts, I said yes.

'I have never been as proud of you as I am today,' Baian said. 'As your mother I could have wished for nothing more than for you to raise a family with Mikael.'

Arrangements were made for our marriage. In the traditional way, it would be in two parts. First would come an Islamic marriage when we would stand before an Imam, a Muslim cleric, and be brought together as man and wife in the eyes of God. Traditionally, we would not sleep together that night. That would come after the second part of our marriage when we would be officially registered, there would be a grand reception and dancing and then we would retire to our bed for the 'deflowering' of the bride. Of course, only Mikael and I knew my shameful secret. I was terrified of what lay ahead. I now knew that close relatives of my family would want evidence that my new husband had taken me. They would want to see blood on the cloth. We would have to fake it.

But as the day of the Islamic marriage approached I kept going back to that fateful chicken and sweet corn evening—I'll always remember it as that. How skilfully Mikael had taken advantage of me. There was no doubt in my mind that he had not been a virgin.

He knew exactly what he was doing. But the male would not be blamed. In Kurdish society I was to learn, it was the woman who would be seen to have done wrong by leading him on. Sex before marriage was *haram* (totally forbidden) and it was always the woman who was the sinner.

Why hadn't my parents explained such things to me and my brother as we grew up in Sydney? My mother, certainly, was very much a part of the burgeoning Kurdish community in Australia to the point of being fanatical about her roots and helping everyone whether they were new arrivals or if there was a need of financial help for some family in far away Kurdistan.

As we stood before the Imam at our family's apartment, with my mother and relatives smiling on, I felt the bitterness coursing through me. I could not face my friends as the day had approached. I was moody, distracted. My mother could see there was something wrong but when she asked I put on a brave smile and told her everything was fine. Even if I had told her what had happened, I knew she would have been shamed and horrified, just as I was, before insisting that I go ahead with the marriage because there would have been no other choice.

The Islamic ceremony, when verses from the Koran were read, was over after an hour and everyone was smiling except for me. There was still the legal side of the wedding to come and I knew I just couldn't face it or the future that lay beyond. I saw myself five years on, burdened by children, my education over, my career not even started and I would still be only 25 years old. My mother had made a career for herself, that was true, after being forced into marriage at the age of 15 but I was living in Europe for heaven's sake. From her teens she had had to carry the responsibility of her children and a husband. She had been able to break away from time to time to go overseas on her own and I wondered just how much she had wished she could stay away and follow whatever path opened for her. But no, she always had had to return home. It was her lot, whether she liked it or not. Her destiny had been shaped in a country far away but she was still tangled in its cultural web.

By a cruel twist of fate—was it a coincidence or were other unknown forces at work?—one of my female cousins who I met at a relative's wedding, told me of news that had come from Kurdistan that very week. It was a terrible story, for the young woman involved, Etab, was not only related to me—I had met her some seven years earlier when my parents had taken me to Kurdistan on a visit. Close to my own age, we had fun as she tried on some of my Western clothing. Her father and my father were blood cousins and although I was too young to understand the implications at the time, I learned after that visit that she had been married off as soon as she had reached puberty.

As beautiful as my friend had been, with fair skin and jet black eyes, a mother of four, she had now been accused of adultery. It seemed that she was a victim of her beauty, for men would follow her and snatch every chance to talk to her. Soon, people began to call her a slut, a whore, to her face. The reality was that her husband had been having an adulterous affair and her unhappiness showed whenever she was out. She was happy to talk to men, for she knew her husband felt nothing for her any more. But her reputation as an 'easy woman' spread and her shamed relatives—my very own relatives—refused to listen to her protests of innocence. One night the men, my father's cousin among them, drove her into the desert, poured gasoline over her and set her alight. As she screamed in agony her husband brought out his gun and ended it with a bullet to her head.

Her grandmother and her mother had been killed for the same reasons. Reputation. Family pride. Honour. Her crime was that she had stopped to talk to a group of men as she went to a well to fetch water. Idle gossip, rumour—and your life could be destroyed.

Thank God I'm here, I thought. How wrong it had been, not only to kill one so young and lovely, but to take a life when the Koran makes it clear that it is wrong to kill something we have not created. No-one can show themselves to be greater than God, the Muslim Holy Book teaches. I have learned things myself from the Koran—although I was not a reader or a follower of its teachings during my time in Australia—the most poignant being that while men who kill those who are younger or more helpless than themselves think they are powerful, such acts are simply showing their weakness.

As arrangements continued for the legal wedding, Mikael and I spent a second time together. I had thought very carefully about it beforehand, believing I should give our relationship another chance in the hope that this time it would be passionate. But I felt nothing. He showed no affection for me and when it was over he was up and out of the room. So this was how it was going to be for years to come, I told myself. No way. Mikael and I had no future as husband and wife.

But who could I turn to for help in escaping from this impending domestic imprisonment?

Finally I made a decision. I was going to let my feelings flow—up to a point. The loss of my virginity would remain my secret, but I would tell my mother what I felt.

'I can't go on with this,' I said when we were in the kitchen. 'I don't love this person. I want to go back to Australia and finish my education, find a career and eventually find someone that I truly love—not someone who sends his mother around to ask you if he can marry me. It's nonsense. That's not love.'

My mother was shocked. Her face fell. She turned her back and put down the cup she had been holding. Silent.

Now I couldn't stop myself. 'I remember you talking to Dad, talking about your treatment by him in Kurdistan and particularly the treatment you received from his mother. You were trapped in his family, looking after them, feeding them, until you were forced to leave.'

Then she spun on me, her face white with anger. But no words came.

'Mum,' I continued, 'I don't want what happened to you to happen to me. If I married Mikael I could end up like you ended up over there in Iraq. I'd be sucked into his family, you know that, and I'd be a slave to their wishes. How do you know, how do I know, that his mother won't make all kinds of demands on me, just like Dad's mother made demands on you?'

She continued staring at me. I could see she was fighting to control an angry outburst. It was the first time I'd talked to her in this way about her life in Iraq. I was preparing myself for a verbal lashing, but instead she said:

'Love comes later. It will come.'

'But with Dad. . . do you really, really love him?'

She stared at me, as if I was a stranger.

'Do not, ever again, talk to me about your father and me. It is none of your business.'

I went to my room and lay on the bed, my mind racing. My mother had dismissed me. I couldn't tell her, I just couldn't. If nothing more, I needed to just talk it over with someone. I felt like my secret was bursting to be released. But who could I talk to? Was there anyone? As just about everyone I knew was connected to the Kurdish community, I realised I had to keep my ordeal to myself. And then I remembered Ojo, my half-German friend.

We met in a café and I told him exactly what had happened. Sadness spread over his face. Sadness for me, or sadness for himself perhaps, because I had sensed in earlier days that he had feelings for me. He reached across the table and touched my hand.

'Latifa,' he said, 'life is much too short for unhappiness. Why would you want to throw away this wonderful gift of life to spend it with someone you will always be unhappy with?'

'But I don't want to let my mother, my whole family, down. The eyes of all my relatives are on me. I can't go this far and back down, surely.'

Now his hand was gripping mine more strongly. 'Your conscience will tell you what to do. And so will your heart.'

He was just a year or two older than me, but he spoke with the wisdom of someone much older. 'Do you want to hear it from me, Latifa? Don't stay with this man. He has abused you. Look at yourself. You are a picture of unhappiness. Where is the laughing, fun girl I've always known? I'm not sitting with her now.'

When I returned home my mother had a surprise for me. And it wasn't nice. 'You will remain indoors with me now until you and Mikael set up your home together as man and wife.'

I watched with growing frustration as my brother went off in the evenings to join his friends, go to parties, to dances, while my mother forced me to remain at home. I paced the lounge room liked a caged tiger.

'What's wrong with you?' Baian demanded. 'Are you on drugs? You're not behaving like my daughter any more.'

'And you're not behaving like my mother,' I raged. Every time I spoke to her, it seemed my frustrations poured out. When I wasn't walking around the room, round and round and round, I was in my bedroom, trying to sleep away my misery. I didn't go to work at our cousin's office. I couldn't face anyone because I knew they would all be looking at me as the bride-to-be and I didn't want to reveal my unhappiness to them.

I couldn't bear the 'cage' that my home had become any more. I packed a bag when my mother and brother were out and fled to Ojo's home. I felt no shame when I went to bed with him. I wanted someone's arms around me. To feel passion—and I did. He cared and I cared. He knew of other Muslim girls in Germany who were trapped like I was about to be, heading towards a marriage I wanted no part of. They were even forced by their parents into praying five times a day in their homes to maintain a good reputation in the Kurdish community—and not particularly for religious reasons. If they weren't at home for any of those prayer sessions, they had to make up for them with 'double prayers' when they got home. I had once asked a cousin whether she was really praying to God or praying just to please her family.

'What do you think?' she said. 'When you have no choice, you just do it.'

When I returned home after staying with Ojo for a few days my mother was silent. I was expecting a furious outpouring, but it never came. But I knew she was containing herself and perhaps it would come later. Little did I realise just how that brewing explosion was to drastically destroy all my hopes of escape from a prison that was closing in around me.

FOUR

My father was coming at me with a knife. His eyes were wild, bloodshot, flamed by vodka.

'Give me your hand!' he demanded. 'I'm going to cut your fingers off! I'll make you scream, my girl. Oh, how I'll make you scream!'

I woke from the nightmare, sweat on my brow. What did it mean? That was not my loving father. I knew I had to call him. My mother and brother had already left for the day and although it was late in the evening in Australia I put the call through.

'Are you all right, Dad?' I asked.

'Yes and no. You know about your mother and me, don't you?'

'No, what?'

I could feel his reluctance to go on. 'We've agreed to separate. Or rather she wants to leave me and I don't seem to have any choice. I won't be coming over to join you.'

I was stunned. There had been no warning of this.

'Oh, Dad,' I cried. 'What happened?' He did not respond. I broke the silence. 'How I wish I could come back to Australia and be with you, pick up where we had left off. I miss you and Sydney so much.'

'Be guided by your mother,' he said. 'We'll meet up soon, don't worry. I'm sure you'll be able to come back here for a holiday or I might be able to get over there.' He seemed strangely distant; something in his voice but I couldn't pick it.

As if I wasn't depressed enough. Now this. Perhaps I should have realised they were going to split up. After all, it had been more than a year since we had left Sydney and there had been no hint that my father was ready to join us. I had assumed that he was still waiting to find a good price for our house.

How dramatically things change. Shortly after that conversation my father was on his way to Germany. But his sudden flight had nothing to do with Baian his wife, or we his children. His younger brother, who lived in Siegen, had been killed in an accident on the autobahn. My father insisted on the body being returned to Kurdistan and, in keeping with culture, he had to be buried within a week. He did not call Baian. Within two days he was on a flight to Iraq with the casket.

My mother's silence was unbearable. Her mood had nothing to do with the separation. She was still furious with me. As each day passed I was waiting for that explosion I knew was coming. I didn't even mention what my father had told me, fearing that she would accuse me of talking about her to my father behind her back.

One day I told her I was going to go out and do some shopping.

'Oh yes, who with?' she asked. 'One of your black friends?'

So that was it. Not only had she wondered where I had been during those missing days, she had since found out about Ojo— when everyone in her family was preparing to welcome me into the

49

community as Mikael's wife. Once or twice I heard her talking on the phone and for some reason I had the impression it was to my father, who was still in Iraq. I heard constant references to 'she. . . she. . . she. . .'

Mikael was constantly 'at me' whenever we travelled to Siegen, talking about the children we would raise and asking which city we would like to settle in. One day the pressure came to a head while we were both attending a wedding.

'We have no future, Mikael,' I said, when we stepped out into a small garden 'Not after what you did.'

'Oh, but we do. How do you think your mother is going to react if I were to tell what happened between us—before any wedding arrangements had been made?'

So it had come to this. Already. My loss of virginity was being used against me. My mind raced. How could I remove this threat? Then it came to me; such a simple response.

'How do you think your family will react if they found out you had comitted a sin? And the police, how will they react when I tell them about your warehouse of stolen goods?' I asked defiantly. 'You've been stupid enough to tell me what you get up to, the drugs, the robberies, the guns. Are you going to risk a jail sentence just to get at me?'

He had no answer to that. He spun on his heel and went inside. I knew my secret was safe with him, but only for as long as I could hold a threat against him.

Before long I was hit with a new shock. But it was a pleasant one—and, most unexpectedly, from my mother. Before I settled down for good in Germany she had been thinking about taking me away for a holiday and now there was some urgency to do this because her father—my grandfather—had taken a turn for the worse. He was in his mid-70s, he was very sick and weak and there were fears he would die any day.

'You know how much he loves you,' she said, reminding me of our earlier visits when he had indeed doted over me. 'He wants to see all his grandchildren before he dies. You need a holiday from all the drama you've been caught up in.'

I couldn't believe my ears. A holiday. The break would put an even greater distance between me and Mikael and in that time my mother would perhaps come to accept that there was no way that she would become a grandmother to his and my children. To add to her good mood, I told her that when we returned to Germany I would make her proud of me and in between 'everything' I would continue my studies. I hoped that would be a hint that I was looking at a career and not settling down with Mikael. She smiled and nodded her head. It was the first time I'd seen her smile in weeks.

I was so sad to hear that my grandfather was dying. It was he, as a schoolteacher, who had taught my mother her English, although I also remembered he had been partly responsible for keeping her at home and marrying her off at a young age. Even so, on those earlier visits, I had enjoyed being with him. He was a jolly man, with a twinkle in his eyes, who threw his big arms around all his grandchildren when they came to visit.

My mother purchased the plane tickets for herself, me and my young sister Bojeen. My brother would not be joining us, she said, because he had to finish his exams. In any case, at the age of 19 he was old enough to look after himself. We would be away for two weeks, although she thought it might be a little longer if her father were to pass away in that time. I sat at the kitchen table looking at the return tickets. I would be free of Mikael's expectations for our future and I knew that soon I would be able to tell him officially it was all over between us.

Shortly before we were due to leave I met Ojo and told him about my grandfather's illness and that I'd be away for a couple of weeks.

'I'll bring you back an *abaia* (a long Arab gown),' I said with a giggle. 'You'll look good walking around Munster in one of those.'

'After everyone's been used to seeing me in jeans, sure,' he said with equal humour. But I saw the tears welling up.

'Don't worry,' I said. 'It's only for a couple of weeks. Then I'll be back with you again. I won't be seeing Mikael, I can assure you of that. You know how I feel about you.'

'I just don't feel good about you going,' he said. 'It just seems so far away.'

'But of course it's not. It's only a few hours. Across Germany to Turkey and then a short drive through the mountains to Kurdistan. I'll call you when I get there.'

It was on 5 June 2001, that my mother, my sister and I took off from Dusseldorf airport to fly to Instanbul. From there, we flew across southern Turkey to the ancient fortress city of Diyarbakir lying north of the mountain ranges separating Turkey from Iraqi Kurdistan. Everywhere I looked in this attractive city, sitting beside the upper reaches of the River Tigris I could see a mosque.

'We're now in Kurdistan,' my mother told me.

'How can we be?' I asked. 'We're still in Turkey, aren't we?'

'We're in Turkish Kurdistan. Our heritage spreads right through this region. The frontiers are drawn up by man. Our culture doesn't recognise such things. Always remember that.'

We remained for two nights in an apartment owned by my mother's friend. She told me she liked to keep a low profile when she was in Turkey and wanted to avoid hotels, but she never explained why. On our last afternoon there she kept Bojeen and me waiting in a park while she went into a café to talk to a number of Turkish men. I could see them at the table talking animatedly but of course she didn't tell me what it was all about.

She woke my sister and me early the following morning, telling us a driver was outside ready to take us to the border, three hours away. Dust flew up behind us as we headed towards our birthplace, Iraqi Kurdistan. We passed through remote villages, heading towards the distant mountains. My mind was everywhere. I was thinking about Germany, Australia and our destination, my mother's home town of Dohuk on the other side of that mountain range. To this day I don't know what inspired me to do it but as we travelled, with my mother in the front of the car with the driver and Bojeen and me behind, I brought out my Australian passport and, using my sister's pencil, wrote down all the details of the photo page on a piece of paper. Not just the passport number, date of issue and expiry, but all the security numbers running along the bottom. Then I tucked that piece of paper into the top of my bra.

In years to come, in 2007, this whole region was to be a war zone, when Turkey launched a massive attack on Iraqi Kurds who were threatening Turkish territory, but now in 2001 the region was peaceful. A special taxi that carried people across 'no man's land' on the frontier brought us to the Iraq border post, which comprised a cluster of buildings. When a guard approached us, my mother instructed him to tell someone inside that she had arrived. Shortly afterwards we were all being escorted into the building, where my mother was met by a large, moustachioed man in his 50s, dressed in a khaki uniform. He greeted her like a long-lost friend, wrapping his big arms around her and kissing her cheeks. I had the impression that he must have lived in the West at some time because no country-bound Kurd would greet a woman that way. How happy he was to see her again, he said in our Kurdish language. She explained that she was going home to see her father who was ill and then gave him my passport and hers, which also contained my sister's name.

When the documents were handed back, I went to take mine but my mother put it straight into her bag. It was the first time she had ever done this on our numerous holiday trips around Europe. When I gave her a questioning look she stared straight back at me, the look of defiance in her eyes worrying me.

We picked up a taxi on the Iraqi side and drove the hour and a half to Dohuk. Why had my mother kept my passport? Did she think I was going to run away from her or something crazy like that? No chance of that—whichever way you looked as we headed towards Dohuk there were only mountains or desert. Why would I run away anyway when I was so anxious to see my grandfather before he died?

The outskirts of the city were vaguely familiar to me, although I hadn't been there for several years since my last holiday. There were still the same old beaten-up cars, the same boring clothing, the women in their headscarfs and long robes and the men in their baggy tracksuit-like pants. My mother did not seem to be interested in the surroundings. She had her head down as we wound through the narrow side streets, her hand pushed through her hair as though she were far away, thinking.

We finally stopped outside a house that I remembered, a large building in the middle of town, very grey and square with a two-metre high brick fence around it, the entrance being a large solid metal door with a peacock emblem. My maternal grandfather's house. The peacock was a symbol of royalty, which was fitting for the birthplace of my mother as she is a descendant of royalty in her tribe, the Sharafani. She was so proud of her heritage that at the radio station in Sydney she would use that name when she introduced herself on air.

I was expecting a sombre mood in the house, where four families, all related to my mother, lived, so I was surprised when the only sounds I heard were the laughter of children from the other side of the wall. We opened the gate and walked into the courtyard, but no-one ran to greet us. It was as though we weren't expected. As it turned out, we weren't.

Then one of my little cousins, his hair red, saw us as we approached the door and ran inside shouting: 'Aunty Baian is here! Aunty Baian is here!' There was an outburst of shrieks. Women came to the door, arms wide to greet us. Followed by my grandfather, someone's baby in his arms. He was the picture of health as he hurried to the door.

Before I hugged him I turned quickly to my mother. 'I thought you said he was very ill.'

She didn't reply and then they were all embracing me and calling my name. But my eyes went back to my 75-year-old grandfather as he clung with powerful arms to my mother. I was witnessing a lie.

'Why didn't you tell us you were coming?' asked one of my aunties. 'We would have prepared a sheep.'

Another lie exposed. My mother had told me we were coming here so we could say goodbye to my grandfather and everyone was expecting us.

'How are you, Granddad?' I had finally found words through my increasing unease.

'Fit as a youngster,' he replied with a roar of laughter. 'God has given me a good life and he hasn't taken his eye off me yet!'

We sat on cushions in a big circle in what I would call the welcoming room, a place set aside for visitors when both men and women of the house could sit in the same room. Later, the women would have to retire to their own room. Tea and pastries and some dips—homous, babaganou—were served but then my mother went out to the kitchen with her older and younger sisters and her sister-in-law. I could hear their voices but could not make out what they were saying. But I could guess what, or rather who, the topic was: me. My mother's behaviour in recent weeks and particularly on this day had been of concern to me and perhaps now the explosion I feared was being suppressed was about to hit me. She had left her handbag in the room. I got up from the circle of children and adults and went over to it, pretending it was mine, and quickly removed my passport. I told everyone I was just popping out to the kitchen and on the way I slipped my passport into my own shoulder bag.

Curiosity about the conversation that was taking place between the women in the kitchen driving me, I walked in on them and asked if there was somewhere I could freshen up. The conversation snapped shut, just like that. They stared at me. Then my mother said:

'I wouldn't bother about that. You're going on to somewhere else.'

'Where? Where am I going?'

She didn't answer but went to our shared luggage bag and started removing her clothes. My address book was in there with all the contact details for my friends in Germany and a few I was occasionally in touch with in Australia. Holding my address book must have triggered a chain reaction of thought for she quickly snatched up her handbag and saw that my passport was missing. She grabbed my shoulder bag and removed it. I tried to grab it back but I was too late.

'Mum, what's going on? What are you doing? Why are you separating our clothes? Why are you keeping my passport? Tell me, for God's sake, tell me!'

'You're going to see your father,' she said.

A wave of relief swept over me. So that was what all the clothes thing was about. She was going to be staying here with her family and I would be staying with my father, now Baian's estranged husband. But my passport and my address book. . .

'Please give them back to me,' I said. 'I want to send postcards to my friends. There are some I might want to ring.' I was, thinking of

Ojo when I said that. I'd promised to call him as soon as I arrived in Kurdistan. But his number was in my address book and apart from needing it to call him, I didn't want my mother snooping through my list of friends. I hadn't written in his name in code or anything. She was bound to see it and although she wouldn't know that he was the 'black friend' she had so venomously referred to, all she needed to do was call that number and she'd soon find out.

'Please give me back my address book and passport,' I implored her once again.

Now she folded her arms and stared at me as everyone in the room watched me. 'You're not going to need your address book. You can forget about everybody who's in it. And you're not going to need your passport either. You're going nowhere. You will now be staying with your father. This is now your home. You will stay here and you will be married here and you will bring up your children here.'

I couldn't believe what I was hearing. Was this my mother speaking to me? Was this another terrible dream, a nightmare like the one I had had with my father coming at me to cut off my fingers? My mouth and my throat were dry. I was being condemned to a life far from everyone I knew and loved. My mother, my very own mother, had tricked me. Betrayed me.

And then, even as I stood there, I was stricken with a fear that I had never felt before. My mother's words of moments ago rushed back at me. *You will stay here and you will be married here and you will bring up your children here.*

Married here. Married here. That simple sentence and its implications terrorised me. I was not a virgin. No-one here knew it. Not even my mother. I wanted to scream it out. But I remembered what had happened to my cousin Etab, how she had been dragged off into the desert and killed. Who knew what would happen were I to cry out then in front of these relatives that I was not 'pure' in their eyes. Would they call for the men to carry me off and end my life, too?

'Come on,' said my mother. 'It's time for you to go to your father. There's a car waiting.'

But I was backing away from the front door, terror driving me towards the kitchen, as far away from this room as I could get. They came towards me, a group of women, hands reaching out for me, to grab me and pull me out of the house. I fell backwards and then I was in the kitchen.

'Don't touch me, don't touch me!' I cried, but their eyes were on me, their hands were reaching out. My own hand brushed something. A knife. I snatched it up in my right hand and turned on them. They stopped dead in their tracks.

And then, as their faces turned white with horror, I held out my left hand and plunged the blade right through my wrist and the blood spurted out at them.

FIVE

The hands that had been reaching for me to pull me into the street now held me as I dropped to my knees on the slate floor. My head was spinning. Someone found a towel and wrapped it around the wound. I saw the knife on the floor, smeared with blood.

Now I was being guided to a room with a bed. The rag was removed and the wound was smeared with ointment. I had missed a vital vein, the blade striking bone and being deflected across the top of my wrist to come out the other side. Straight through.

I wanted my mother to see my pain, feel my pain. Not just from the injury but my internal agony. She was among the group who stood around the bed looking down on me as the wound was wrapped in another piece of cloth, but she said nothing.

'Let me see my grandfather,' I said. He was already at the door, peering in.

'I'm here.'

'Grandfather,' I implored, remembering that the eldest in the family had the final say. 'They want to keep me here. They are not going to let me go back to Germany or home to Australia. Please help me. Please tell them they can't do this. I'm almost 21. I'm a grown woman. I'm an Australian citizen. I've been tricked into coming here. My mother—' I turned my head towards her—'told me you were sick, asking for me. And look at you. There's nothing wrong with you. Doesn't that tell you something?'

He looked embarrassed, clearly unwilling to be drawn into this. Perhaps in his silence he was acknowledging the power my mother held in the family. A couple of hours earlier he had been playing with his young nieces and nephews and his great grandchildren and now he was being confronted with a Western girl who had stabbed herself in the arm and was crying out to be taken home.

Tears poured down my face at his silence, for he knew he was clearly outnumbered. I had come all the way from Germany just to be with him in what I had been told was his hour of need, yet all he could do now was stand in silence when I needed him. Then I saw my little sister pushing her way through the women. She was crying too, confused by all the commotion, by my outburst.

One of the women turned to my mother: 'She can't go when she's like this. We should let her rest for a while.'

An aunt sat in the room with me—a guard?—as the others left and I closed my eyes. I could feel the wound throbbing but it was nothing to the turmoil in my head. How could my mother have done this—lure me here on false pretences and then tell me that this country was to be my home for the rest of my life? While those thoughts sickened me, I wondered just how long the rest of my life would be. If they forced me into a marriage that really would be the end of me, if those honour-killing stories were true. Again, I thought of my cousin Etab, burned alive and shot. Was that to be my fate when any husband forced upon me found out that I was not a virgin? My mind went back to that 'chicken and corn soup evening' and I felt Mikael's hand over my mouth as he clambered onto me, a naive woman who should have known what was happening—but didn't until it was too late. Too late for ever.

It must have been an hour before I felt strong enough to get up from the bed and make my way to the bathroom. My baby sister rushed towards me, wrapping her arms around my legs, too young to understand what was happening but knowing that something was terribly wrong.

I threw water on my face, hoping it would wake me from a nightmare but when I opened my eyes I was still standing in the drab bathroom and my blood was seeping through the rag around my wrist.

'This is not going to change anything.'

It was my mother's voice. She was at the bathroom door. 'Your position remains the same. You can threaten to throw yourself from the roof or under a car, but I will not change my mind.'

This wasn't my mother. What had happened to her? I had nothing to say. If plunging the knife into my arm could not persuade her to let me go home, words would fail miserably. By now it was late in the afternoon. My luggage had been repacked and was by the door. One of my aunties offered me some food. Now I turned on her, for I saw everyone in this room, except my little sister, as the enemy.

'Why should I eat with any of you? Don't any of you realise what you are doing? You are holding me as a prisoner and that's against the law.'

They didn't know what I was talking about. I swung around to my mother. I would embarrass her in front of this family of hers.

'Not only have you betrayed me, you also betrayed my dad. Don't think that I didn't know you were seeing other men behind his back in Australia. You're a wicked woman and these relatives of yours should know about it.'

Their eyes darted from me to her. If looks could kill I would have dropped dead right then. It was obvious that none of them believed me, that this was an outpouring of rage from a daughter who could not be controlled. God only knows what she had told them, her sisters, about me as I lay in that bedroom.

'Let's go,' one of them said now. 'It will be better if you leave before darkness comes.'

A male cousin, who had been waiting outside with the car and who, like my grandfather had not wanted to interfere, picked up my luggage and led me out. I begged my mother to let me take my sister Bojeen with me, just for an hour, and I would send her back. Amazingly, she agreed.

Since my parents had fled from my father's family home in Mosul 21 years earlier when he had learned our names were on an execution list, my father's family had moved to Dohuk. So now my father was also living in Baian's home town, following his arrival in Kurdistan with the body of his brother who had been killed in the autobahn accident. The split with my mother and the fact that his own children had been living with her in Germany had left him with only loneliness in Australia, so when he brought his brother's body to Kurdistan he decided to stay, living with his grief-stricken mother. Our former home in Sydney's west had been sold and the money had been transferred to Baian's bank in Germany before my parents had agreed to go their separate ways. He was to learn later what a mistake that had been.

It was just a 10-minute drive to my father's house but I took no notice of the route. I clutched six-year-old Bojeen's hand as the tears ran down my face. She was frightened.

'What's happening? Why are you crying? Why were you and Mummy shouting?'

She fired her little girl's questions at me but I had no easy answers that would console her. I tried to explain that I would be staying with our father while she enjoyed the two-week holiday with our mother. But I assured her, and I had no doubt about this, that I would be seeing a lot of her in coming days.

We pulled up outside a one-storey house with a two-metre high fence around it, just like the home of my mother's family and typical of so many of the houses in Dohuk. The leaves of a fig tree hung over into the street. I was filled with trepidation. I hadn't seen my father since 1998—three years earlier, when we had moved to Germany. Then the big iron gate swung open to the toot of our car and there he was, my father Khalid with his familiar bushy, dark eyebrows. His once-iron-grey hair was heading towards white and it was a little thinner in front, but nothing else about him seemed to have changed at all. At least not in appearance. Oh, how appearances could deceive.

'Welcome home, my first child,' he said in the traditional greeting as he embraced me. He did not see the makeshift bandage around my wrist because I was wearing long sleeves. He had obviously been expecting me but I was to find out that there was no phone in the house so there would have been no opportunity for my mother to call him to tell him that I had stabbed myself. He smothered Bojeen in his arms while the cousin who had brought us watched without a smile. I was expecting him to say something about my injured arm, but he remained silent, and perhaps they hadn't told him about the incident.

'Have you brought enough clothes?' Khalid asked as he ushered me and Bojeen inside. 'I don't know what your mother has said, but you'll be staying here for a while and then, when I've saved enough money, we'll be going back to Australia.'

My heart leaped. 'When? When will that be?'

'I can't say just yet. Just trust me.'

It was then that I noticed his mother, my grandmother, Aisha, stepping towards us. Age was written in wrinkles across her face, although she was still only in her early 60s. You could see her Arab background in her charcoal hair and crossed eyebrows. Her palid skin gave the appearance of having never received the tiniest ray of sunlight. She shuffled towards me, grim-faced and gave me a quick kiss on the cheek, more out of formality than affection, it seemed. But then, she had never liked me or my brother because we were our mother's children and she hated Baian. Even worse, she detested my sister because she had my mother's features. I had always thought it sad, hearing my mother talking about her husband's mother over the years as she reflected on the hatred that Aisha held for her. I could not understand why Baian had given her son a child—me— at the earliest opportunity after her marriage to him, yet my birth had failed to win the approval, not to mention love, of Aisha.

She was dressed in black, still grieving over the death of her younger son in the autobahn accident. But her sullen expression was how I always remembered her from our earlier visits to Kurdistan. Seeing her now added to my depression. It was just her and my father living in this house and I wondered how I would be able to face the days, weeks—not months, surely not, dear God—ahead. I wondered what Ojo would be thinking if he could see me now, preparing to settle in with this surly woman and my father when just a few days earlier I had set out happily from Germany, telling him I would call, that I would miss him, and that I'd be back in a couple of weeks. Even as they started showing me around the house, I recalled reservations Ojo had about me going to Kurdistan and unfairly felt a flash of anger. If he had believed something was wrong, why didn't he try to stop me? Why didn't he say something like: 'If you go, I won't be here for you when you come back.' Such were the thoughts that struck me in those first minutes of being in my surly grandmother's company but they were panic thoughts as I sought to cast blame on anyone I could think of for my predicament.

My father talked playfully with Bojeen for a while, gave her a cold drink and then it was time for her to be taken back to the other house. I held her tight and the tears flowed down both our faces—hers because she was still confused and scared by all that had happened in the past hours; mine because I had no idea when I would see her again.

The room they gave me was filled with bedroom furniture that my parents had when they were living in Mosul. The bed, the dressing table with the large round mirror above, the closet with the lace curtain across the front, had all belonged to them.

The rest of the house comprised a men's room, where there was a TV—the house had four TVs in fact, all connected to very parochial local channels—and a sofa and many cushions; a women's room which was stark with a few mats and cushions scattered around; my grandmother's room; and finally my father's room. There was a kitchen and a bathroom where the 'shower' consisted of a stool on which the user sat and poured water over himself or herself with a plastic saucepan-like ladle. There was no window as such in my room, although there was a narrow glass opening on the top of one wall dividing my room from a small storage room and the kitchen beyond. All the main windows of the house were protected by vertical iron bars.

Depression swept over me and I asked to be excused for the night, even though it was still early evening. My arm hurt. My head ached. Some holiday this had turned out to be, I told myself, trying to cheer myself up with black humour but it didn't work. Finally I dropped off to sleep and did not wake until noon the following day. My grandmother and father offered me lunch of biryani—rice with nuts and currants—along with lamb stew and platefuls of meat; an important part of Kurdish culture. There was also the traditional round, flat, Middle Eastern bread; and a salad of cucumbers and onions mixed with lemon juice. Then I returned to my room and lay on the bed, my thoughts taking me back to Australia, to Germany, to the faces of my friends. My friends! My mother had even taken my contact book. I felt totally isolated and remembered little of that day until darkness came and sleep carried me away.

The following day my mother's sisters and numerous cousins stopped by to say hello and drop off some clothes I had left behind. I felt I had to put on the appearance of being in a happier mood and in fact I had hope in my heart that they had come to pick me up. But that was not to be. They would have known how miserable I was from my antics of two days earlier, but they said nothing about it. They didn't even ask how my arm was, although the bandage around it was obvious to them. My face probably revealed how heavy my heart was. How could anyone expect me to be happy living in a shoebox of a house with my father who now seemed strangely different—and I was soon to find out why—along with a grandmother who clearly hated me, and a cluster of TVs.

'I think I might go outside for a while,' I told them.

Heads shook. 'You can't go out,' one of my aunties said. 'The boys from next door are on their roof. They'll be able to look down and see you.'

'What do you mean, they'll be able to see me? I'm not going out naked, you know.'

My words shocked them. In time I found out why. Any unmarried woman—any teenager beyond puberty, in fact—who shows her face to a man when she is not accompanied by a married person is considered a whore. There would be no strolls down to the shops on my own for me. Gracious, I couldn't even go out into the garden if those boys next door were out and about. I really was a prisoner of this cloistered culture and as time went by I was to find out just how torturous this life was for a girl who had grown up under the big blue skies of Australia.

On the fourth day I asked my visiting aunties if I could go and visit my sister, or whether she could come to see me. What they said left me reeling.

'You can't see her. Bojeen and your mother left today.'

'Left? Left for where?'

'They've gone home. Back to Germany.'

I didn't know whether to laugh or cry. The betrayal was complete. I realised now that my mother had planned this all along. This was the real explosion, erupting right now with those words: 'They've gone home.'

It never was to be a holiday. It was a trip to dump me in northern Iraq, where the rebellion I had shown over settling down with a Kurdish man in Germany would be put down. This mother of mine, so fanatical about her people, had been determined that I would become one of them and my denial of Mikael had clearly angered her. I would become a good Muslim girl. A marriage would be arranged if I did not find a husband for myself.

But my mother's action was a double betrayal, although she was not to know that.

For she had placed me under a death sentence. Any future husband would discover I was not a virgin and I had little doubt that my cries of 'I'm an Aussie! We are free people!' would be no defence against the fatal punishment that would be handed down to me.

If I had any hope that there might be someone in the family who

I could come to trust and reveal my secret, that was soon destroyed. Without so much as a 'by your leave' my grandmother and three of my aunties, my father's sisters, came into my bedroom one afternoon while I was trying to sleep away my misery and threw back the lace curtain, beyond which my clothes were hanging. They began taking my low-cut tops off hangers and raising them aloft as they tutted at the 'disgraceful' styles. There was worse to come. They pulled back a small drawer and brought out my lacy bras and my brief underwear.

'Just look at this!' one of them exclaimed. 'These are the garments of a slut.' Their mocking laughter filled the room.

They turned to me. 'These will be destroyed. You will be given more appropriate clothing.'

As they pulled more of my clothes out my grandmother, who had slipped away, returned with a pair of scissors and I watched in disbelief as she began cutting everything to ribbons. As the pieces fell to the floor and one of my aunties kicked them towards the door I felt too numb to react.

'And look at these,' said an aunt, holding up a pair of my black pants. 'They are so ridiculously tight I might have trouble fitting just one leg into them!'

'Disgraceful. Is this what she wears all the time?'

'What about this brassiere. Just look at how low cut it is.'

'If she wore that with this top, people would see everything.'

'She's a disgrace. We'll have to change her attitude.'

I could take the insults no longer. I jumped up from the bed.

'Leave my things alone,' I cried. 'You have no right. Have you no respect for other people's property?'

'Not this stuff. Is this what you've been wearing?'

'All of you can talk. Just look at the drabby old things you've got on. And when did you last wash it? It's covered in dust.'

My father stepped into the room. Thank God. He would take my side now because he knew how much I loved shopping for nice things when we were living in Sydney. But he was looking at me darkly.

'Don't answer back. Don't turn into your mother.'

His words frightened me. Not just the fact that he was supporting these crones who were tearing my clothes to pieces but because, for the first time, he was exposing his true feelings about my mother. They had decided to go their separate ways, that was true, but I had never heard him criticise her in that way.

Even as he stood in the doorway witnessing the desecration of my property I saw one of my aunties pull a German teenage girls' magazine from my bag. It had photographs of young women of my age modelling the latest fashions. It was flung out through the door, just missing my father. Amazingly, though, they did not touch my Walkman and a couple of my CDs featuring my favourite singer, Tracy Chapman, whose music had been a part of my life since I was eight. In the days to come, her songs were to help me keep my sanity.

It was obvious my father had become very much a part of his family—the way he sided with my aunties against me was evidence of that—but there was something else about him that was staring me in the face, yet it hadn't sunk in. Then as the end of that first depressing week approached he came into my room early in the morning and woke me.

'Aren't you going to pray?' he asked as I wiped the sleep from my eyes.

'Pray? We never prayed in Australia.'

'We're not in Australia. I thought you might have realised that by now.'

'Oh, I realise that all right.'

'And don't answer back. You're always answering back. I've asked you a question. You should now start praying like every true Muslim.' He left, leaving me to lie there, staring at the ceiling.

Of course, that was it. The hard-drinking, chain-smoking father I'd known in Sydney had been 'converted' back to his true faith. I don't know whether he prayed five times a day when he was brought up here in Kurdistan and was living in the mountains as a freedom fighter before I was born because the subject never arose as I was growing up in Australia. But the strange difference I had noticed in my father when I first arrived had suddenly become obvious to me. He had stopped drinking, although he was still smoking. And he was often absent from the main living room, retiring, I now realised, to his own bedroom to pray. Well, I had never been brought up to pray five times a day and I certainly had no intention to start now. They wouldn't force their religion onto me. No-one had the right to do that.

Later that day, with several of my aunties present, he once again raised the topic of my having to pray, telling me that there was only one God and that I should live a life of purety and forsake all the wickedness that had previously surrounded me. I couldn't believe I was hearing this because my father had loved his lifestyle in Australia. I wondered how a man could change so quickly. It was as though he had been struck by a blinding light and his eyes had been opened to a different world. I later learned the reason for his change—the death of his brother. He had suddenly been confronted by his own mortality. He had seen plenty of death in his younger days as he had fought for Kurdistan's freedom, but with his arrival in Australia with us, his young family, he had left it all behind. His brother's death, however, had hit him hard. Returning to Kurdistan with the body and participating in the funeral and the accompanying prayers had opened the door again to his devotion to God.

Now he was trying to convert me. Well, that wasn't going to happen. I was determined to get out of this place as soon as possible. Not only because of the religious pressures that my father and his female relatives were putting on me, but principally because of the terrible secret of my lost virginity. If those women ever found out about 'my condition' I had no doubt they would hurl me out into the street, while the men in the family would ensure that I 'disappeared' before the shame I had brought to their doorstep spread around the neighbourhood and the city.

'You are letting your father down with your attitude,' my grandmother told me one morning as I washed the breakfast plates in the kitchen. This was a task I didn't mind. It gave me something to do.

'What attitude?' I asked. 'You're the one with attitude. You've ripped up my clothes and you've made it perfectly clear that you hate the sight of me. Well, if you hate me so much, why don't you let me go home?'

Her lips tightened and she turned and shuffled out into the living room. I heard her talking to my father, her only remaining son.

Then I felt his presence behind me—and the next moment my hair was in his fist, my head was yanked back, I was spun around and he slapped me hard across the face.

'Don't ever answer back to your grandmother again,' he snapped. 'You will show her respect.'

'She's just like her mother,' said my grandmother, standing behind him. 'She will harm you unless you control her.'

I was too shocked for tears. My face was burning from the blow. My voice trembled as I looked into his dark eyes.

'You are not the father I knew. My father would never strike me. My father was a good man. You are the devil.'

I braced myself for another fierce slap, but it didn't come. He turned and walked away, his mother shuffling behind him.

My father had seven sisters. One was in Germany, another was in Baghdad and the third was in the States. The remaining four were here in Dohuk. Unless I could escape, I feared that those women, under my grandmother's archaic governance, would be the death of me.

SIX

I slipped into a boring routine, sleeping at every opportunity, escaping from my real, depressing world into a happier world of dreams. I saw myself in the fun times; going out with friends and hearing their laughter. I would not even step from my bedroom until midday when I would eat a little lunch, before returning to my bed. I had not been outdoors since I arrived. They were afraid of me being seen by the boys next door and as for strolling down the street just to stretch my legs, that was entirely out of the question.

I begged my father to let me go shopping, even if it was just for household things but he said it was impossible for me to go alone. When I asked him to come with me he said a father and daughter never went shopping together.

'But don't you even remember how we used to do that in Australia?'

He dismissed the memory, declaring: 'And what a waste of time that was.'

'Are you saying that our life in Sydney was one big lie? That you hated it all there? Is this why my mother decided to run away to Germany from you and why you've now split up?'

This was a severe 'answer back'. He slapped me across the face again and told me not to be so insolent. I was approaching my 21st birthday, virtually a legal adult and long past being a minor. But those were Western ideals. Nothing like that worked here. I was my father's daughter and I was in his house and if he wanted to slap me he considered that his right.

'Forget about Australia,' he said. 'You aren't going back.'

'How strange that you should have told me when I first came here to this house that it would be only for a while and then you and I would be returning to Sydney. My father has not only turned into a bully, he's also a liar, a liar to his own daughter.'

He struck me again

'You can go on hitting me, Dad,' I said. 'You won't change my attitude to anything. You raised me as an Aussie kid and a Western woman and now, in the bat of an eyelid, you are trying to make me like you.'

'Don't continue with this,' he said and walked away.

My defiance angered his mother even more. While my father's sullen face turned to smiles whenever his sisters called by, his mother's evil glances towards me were constant. 'You're behaving like a devil,' she told me one day when I answered her back. 'You are just like your mother.'

'No,' I retorted. 'I am not just like my mother. I haven't betrayed anyone, but I've seen how it's done.'

'This obstinate behaviour of yours will not be allowed to continue,' she said, her voice harsh. 'You will begin to say your daily prayers and you will respect your God.'

'If it means finding someone to respect I will turn to God, because I can't find any respect for you,' I told her. She repeated my words to my father. He came at me in a rage and once again I felt his hand slash across my face.

My bedroom became my only escape. A prison within a prison. My pillow was wet with my tears. My injured arm was still painful to the touch although the wound was closing with daily doses of ointment that one of my aunties brought around.

The only relief through my despair was the thought that my estranged parents had not lined me up for marriage with anyone—yet. That was obviously the plan, for they had both threatened me with it. But I was determined I would not be forced into anything. Could I get out of this terrible place—such a beautiful country yet such a miserable existence for me within it—before I was dragged into a marriage that would almost certainly end, not in immediate divorce, but in my death? My thoughts went daily to Ojo back in Germany. I wondered what he must be thinking. The days had gone by and there had been no contact from me. Apart from there being no phone in the house I couldn't even remember his phone number—it was in my contact book. I had no access to the internet to send him an email. There was an internet café in the town, I later learned, but it was full of men and I would never be able to go in there on my own.

I considered making a break for it. Pleading with someone to take me to the border where I could beg lifts to Ankara or Instanbul in Turkey or Tehran in Iran and where I'd be able to reach an Australian embassy. What fanciful thinking that was. I didn't even have a passport. And who was going to say, 'Oh hello, young lady, you who are trying to tell me you are from Sydney and asking for a lift to the border. Yes, of course I'll take you. Doesn't matter if your father or his cousins find out and kill me. I'll take you. No, it doesn't matter that you don't have any money. I'll take you to the border for nothing.'

Some hope. Yes, I had my passport details scribbled on a piece of paper and a scrawled note stating when I had arrived in Kurdistan but that was no ticket to freedom. Whichever way I looked, there was no way out. No contact with the outside world. Outside world? I didn't even have any contact with the people in the street.

What inspired me to write those passport details on a slip of paper? Perhaps I had subconsciously recalled my father's story from years before of how he had written his personal details on a piece of paper and carried it in his shoe—a practice that had resulted in us fleeing from Kurdistan in the first place.

The weeks rolled by and more grim news came from the lips of my father.

'Do you know what that mother of yours, has done?' He asked. How I could hear my hated grandmother in that tone of voice. 'Not only has she filed for divorce, she has given all the money from the sale of our house in Sydney to her brothers, so they can buy land here in Kurdistan. That money was to be for you and your brother, for your education. It was to help your brother in Germany and it was to see you through university and beyond, here.'

The only words that really sank in at that moment were 'university and beyond, here.' Again, an assumption that my future lay in Kurdistan.

My father was speaking again. 'This is the pay-off for her brothers to accept our divorce. The block of land will be divided into three and they will be building their houses on it. And from there they can sit back and laugh at me.'

He explained that no-one in Kurdistan could seek a divorce unless the family approved for there was great shame in a couple separating. If adultery by the wife was concerned it could be quickly settled with a bullet in her head and if it was adultery by the husband and he wanted to start a new life with another woman, the deserted wife's family would have to receive compensation. That way, any shame would be 'bought off'. But it was my mother who had filed for divorce from far away. If she had tried it in Kurdistan, well, she was smart enough not to even mention it in Dohuk.

'That's your mother for you,' my father continued. 'She had this planned all along.'

'Yes,' I said, 'and that's not all she had planned. She very carefully schemed for me to be dumped on you. If you are so much against her now, perhaps you will see my side of things.'

'Her position and your position in my life are separate. The only link is that you are her daughter.'

'And I'm your daughter, too.'

But my argument was in vain. I had sensed my grandmother's venom in his words. She was obviously a great influence over him and she had made it very clear so many times how much she despised my mother. People had remarked to me in the past that I had my mother's walk, I was tall like her and I had her laugh, although I didn't have her looks. That didn't make any difference to my paternal grandmother. I was Baian's offspring and that was enough.

I had thought that if I could show to my aunties photos of me in Sydney and Germany they would understand something of the life they were pulling me away from and that Kurdistan was not the place for me to be. Such thoughts evaporated, though, as I realised that I really had no hope of influencing people who had never had a taste of the West, but I also remembered that my mother had not only stolen my passport and contact book but all my personal photos that I had planned to show to my relatives during my brief 'holiday' among them.

My father's sisters were still entering my room and looking

through my belongings. I was being driven to despair by their rudeness and in a fit of anger I railed on my father. 'Please tell your fat ugly sisters to stop invading my privacy.'

I braced myself for another blow, but this time it didn't come. He just walked away to his room to say his prayers.

I was putting on weight. The food my grandmother and sometimes her daughters prepared was oily, heavy, lots of meat and bread. And I was getting no exercise, apart from walking from my room to the reception room, to the bathroom and back again, to sleep. Once or twice, when the coast was clear, I was allowed to step out into the garden, where there was a small lawn and the fig tree that I had first noticed when I arrived, but if any of the young men next door were sitting on their roof, which they often did, I had to go back inside immediately. Even if I covered my hair and wore a long neck-to-ankle dress, my grandmother and my aunties considered I would be flaunting myself.

One grand and glorious day, one of my aunties said they were taking me into town to do some shopping. I couldn't believe my ears. I was going to go shopping! Such an everyday event in Australia, but for me now it was a special treat. I put on another long gown, tucked my long dark hair under a scarf and climbed into one of two taxis with a couple of my aunts and their daughters. The town was bustling, but I saw mostly men. The narrow, crowded streets of the town twisted and turned in all directions, the roads pitted with potholes, the kerbsides shattered. Some places looked like they had been bombed, although they hadn't been. It was simply neglect. I saw mostly men. I couldn't help noticing when we left the taxi the way they stared at me, undressing me with their eyes, cigarettes hanging from their lips. I was soon to experience my first case of sexual harassment—as we moved though one of the narrow streets, filled with the redolence of perfumes and spices and alive with the blaring of car horns, I felt fingers pinch my bottom. I turned angrily, but it was impossible to identify the culprit in the crowd. I cried out to one of my cousins, when I felt the 'nip' but she urged me to lower my voice and not make a fuss.

'Just pretend nothing happened,' she said.

What women I did see were in three classes—Muslims like my aunties, clothed from head to toe; Assyrians who were Catholics and not expected to wear the *hijab*, the headscarf; and finally the women who, while single and still virgins, wore Western-style clothes. Even those were in groups of two or three. No woman was alone.

'Those,' said my aunt 'are the sluts of our city. We are going to make certain you never end up looking like them.'

'What do you mean "looking like them"?' I asked. 'That's what I've always looked like. Dear God, they're not even wearing make-up, they're not wearing high heels, they're just wearing knee-length skirts. And you're calling them sluts. Let me dress like I used to in Sydney and I'll give you "slut".'

Another angry outburst that shocked them. But I had to fight this. In fact, I wasn't fighting out of defiance. It was a natural reaction, a defence of me!

'Do you know what my father—your dear, devoutly religious brother—did in Australia? He let me wear a bikini! Do you know what a bikini is? It shows my legs—all of my legs!—it shows my bare stomach and it shows my cleavage right down to my nipples!'

We began shopping in a fabric store, bursting with fabulous silks of every colour under the rainbow. I felt like I was stepping through a Bollywood movie, such was the array of brilliant cloths. Among the items we bought, on instructions from my father, were more long dresses for me. In the house I was allowed to wear long pants but because I was putting on weight, my father told me that he would not allow the shape of my behind to show, so he now wanted me to wear a dress over the top of my pants. This was the father who had allowed me to wear skimpy swimming costumes in Australia. I suspected, again, that his mother was the cause of these strict house rules but then, he had changed so much that perhaps this was his idea anyway.

How curious, I had begun to so often think, that mothers were so keen for their sons to marry, yet when they did there was a resentment towards the new wife because she was taking the son away. I certainly suspected that was the case with my father and his mother. And those poor girls who were married off may have hoped that they were going to have a life of freedom and love and wealth, but it lasts just a few days. At least, that is the case with 85 per cent of them: a deflowering on the wedding night and then it's off to the husband's family home and straight into a life of slavery, doing the cooking, the cleaning and caring for the husband's parents.

Escape was constantly on my mind. Getting across the frontier into either Turkey or Iran—the closest borders—were out of the question without a passport and, I decided after thinking about it more carefully, I would be risking my life to try anything like that alone, even if I did have a passport. No, the only obvious way out of there was to try to reach Baghdad, where I could tell the Australian Embassy about my plight. They would be under an obligation to help once I requested assistance. I knew that travelling there on my own would be impossible. For a start, I didn't even have any money, to say nothing of the difficulties of a woman travelling on her own unless she was old. Then a glimmer of hope arose.

One of my father's sisters, Hadar, who lived in Baghdad, came to Dohuk for a visit with her tall, handsome husband Abdullah who worked as a driver for the UN World Food Programme. A part-time teacher, Hadar was the only one of Khalid's sisters to whom I took a liking. She was polite to me and I suspected, coming as she did from a big city where she was used to seeing foreign women, she realised how trapped I felt. She would be unlikely, I rightly believed as it transpired, to raise the matter with my father. I could not tell her my secret, either. In this dangerous land, that secret really would remain with me.

What I was correct in assessing about Hadar was that she saw my misery and felt for me. She suggested to her brother, my father, that I travel back to Baghdad with her and her husband for a short break of a week or so. To my astonishment, he agreed. I realised that he knew Hadar could not afford to let him down in any way. Before we left, the ground rules were laid down. As we would be travelling south out of Kurdistan and into Iraqi territory, where Arabic was spoken, I had to ensure I did not speak in public. Although I did not speak much Arabic in any case, any attempt would reveal my Kurdish accent, mixed perhaps with a slight Aussie twang, although no-one would really know what that was! What anyone overhearing me might assume, however, was that I was a spy, or certainly that there was something curious about me. There were big rewards on offer for the capture of spies acting against Saddam Hussein's regime. I looked Arabic, yet I had a 'strange' accent, it might be said, and the authorities would be upon me in a flash. That might be a good thing, I thought, because I would be able to explain that I was an Australian woman. On the other hand, that could make it even worse, for what was an Australian doing speaking Kurdish? And where, they would ask, were my documents, my passport, to prove who I was? How suspicious it would look when I told them that I didn't have a passport. They would ask for a home address and find out I was living with a father for whom there had been an execution warrant years before, a man who was an enemy of Iraq. Now they had his daughter, who with her father, had fled the region, even though I was just a child of two. They could use my capture to get

81

to my father. Even though he had turned so violently against me, I could not allow that to happen.

Such thoughts raced through my mind as we made preparations to travel to Baghdad. I would have to remain as quiet as a mouse—unless I could somehow reach someone at the Australian Embassy.

It was a hot summer day when we set off for the six-hour drive to Baghdad. I remained in the car when we stopped for fuel on the Arabic, Iraqi, side of the border. I didn't even dare go to the toilet. I managed to avoid that until we at last reached the upper-class Monsour district of Baghdad, where Hadar and her family lived in a neat, white-painted house, again surrounded by a security wall.

They settled me in to my room before I took myself off to the bathroom for a shower. As was the custom, I undressed in the bathroom—rather than throwing a towel around myself as I had always done in Australia and Germany—and let the water run down over my body. It was a proper shower, not like the plastic saucepan I had been using in Dohuk. I slipped back into a long kaftan and walked down the passageway to drop the damp towel in a laundry room. Suddenly I was aware of a movement behind me and then I felt hands reach around and brush against my breasts. I spun around. Abdullah was standing there, grinning.

'Just checking if you enjoyed your shower,' he said. 'Did you rub yourself all over, like this'—and he then ran his hands up and down his own chest, around his legs and his crotch. I stared at him in horror. I wanted to scream out but somehow I retained my silence. The last thing I needed to do was bring Hadar running and cause conflict between her and her husband. No doubt she would have heard claims that I was a 'troublemaker' from that terrible mother of hers in Dohuk and my claims of assault—which Abdullah would undoubtedly deny—would turn her, my only friend, right against me. So I kept my mouth shut. I brushed past him, trying to convince myself that perhaps it had started out as a joke with him and he had gone a little further than he intended. In any case, I didn't want to create a barrier between him and me. He had a car, he could drive me around Baghdad and perhaps he could get me close enough to the Australian Embassy for me to run out and ask for help. Wild thoughts, but I was desperate.

Hadar took me into central Baghdad the following day and it was such a relief to be able to visit shops without a whole gang of aunties or cousins surrounding me as they had in Dohuk. In one shop I stopped in amazement. On display were a row of small toy koalas. I almost cried out to Hadar: 'Look, koalas from Australia!' But I stopped myself just in time. Such an outburst would have drawn immediate attention to me. As it was, I didn't really like them. They were dark brown and the shape was wrong but then again they were Iraqi koalas!

The following day Abdullah offered to take me into town with him. In Baghdad it was unlikely that a man travelling with a woman in a *hijab* and kaftan would attract any attention, for it would be assumed they were man and wife. Abdullah would have been able to explain to any workmates who saw us that I was a relative, which was true. I just had to make sure I kept my mouth shut.

As we crawled through the traffic towards central Baghdad I worked out a plan. I would slowly bring him around to the fact that I wanted to go to the Australian Embassy—'just for a look'.

Whenever we saw anything that symbolised the West, a Pepsi sign and even a company car with English writing, I would make what I hoped would be an innocent comment like: 'That reminds me so much of Australia.' I started telling him about Sydney, the bridge, the Opera House, and he started asking me more questions. This was exactly what I wanted—because then I suddenly said: 'Hey, Abdullah, are we anywhere near the Australian Embassy?

I'd so love to see that, too, just to look at the flag because it would remind me so much of where I used to live a long time ago.' Again, I was trying to subtly distance myself from my home country, yet trying to get close to the Embassy. Would I make a break for it then—jump out of the car and dash to the gates and beg to be let in?

Abdullah interrupted my thoughts. 'You just want to look at a flag? That's stupid. Don't you know what the flag looks like?'

'Yes, of course, but I also thought that I might even hear some Australian voices. It would make me feel so good to hear them after all this time. Surely there would be no harm in that?'

He took his eyes off the road for a moment as we sat in yet another traffic jam. 'So, you're going to walk up to a security guard sitting on the gate outside the embassy and ask him if you can listen to someone speaking Australian? Are you crazy? For a start, he's not going to let anyone get anywhere near the people inside unless they have an appointment or a specific reason. And no-one is going to wander out into the street and start talking to a stranger like you. They come and go out of that building in their vehicles. What are you going to do, flag them down and say "Speak to me, speak to me, I want to hear your voice?"'

He ranted on. 'There's also the security guard. If you speak to him, he's going to know you aren't an Iraqi. He might not think anything of it, but then again he might just take the number of my car and report us to the secret police. No Latifa, forget all about the Australian Embassy.'

Another hope had been dashed. He was right. Approaching the Embassy in person out of the blue, me a woman, was fraught with difficulties. Now a new problem lurked. On the way back to the house, Abdullah kept glancing at me. Or rather my breasts. Once or twice his hand brushed against my thigh as he changed gears. I turned my legs as close as I could towards the door. The closest I came to saying anything was: 'Please be careful', when he did it again. I didn't want to distance him too much—I might still need him because I was in Baghdad, away from my father and my grandmother and the closest I had come to 'freedom' since my arrival.

The sexual harassment did not stop. It worsened. Whenever Hadar was at work, or in the kitchen, Abdullah would, without apology, grab my kaftan and jerk it up to look at the lower part of my legs. Every time he looked at me, I could sense him undressing me with his eyes. After a few days of this, I could not take it any more. I was bursting to tell my aunt what was happening, but the thought of being branded a marriage wrecker, or at least someone who had tried to be one, forced me to hold my tongue. I had been so desperate to come to Baghdad and now I found myself longing for the day when I could return to Dohuk, away from my letcherous uncle's hands.

As that day finally approached, when it had been arranged with my father for my return, there was bad news.

'I can't go with you,' Hadar said. 'I can't get the time off for another week. You'll have to go with Abdullah.'

The thought of travelling alone with Abdullah for the six hour journey to Dohuk appalled me. I had visions of being driven onto a desert road to some lonely place and being raped. I had no hesitation in thinking that if I were alone with him, that is what would happen and who would believe me when I reported it? Me, the trouble-maker. Me, who my grandmother hated so much. Me, for whom my father held so much displeasure. They would all take the side of my uncle—and if that rape did happen, he would find out that I was not a virgin. Then he would have a hold over me for all time. He could demand sex every time the opportunity arose against a threat of spreading the word. I was condemned no matter how I looked at it. How was I to avoid travelling to Dohuk alone with him?

SEVEN

Perhaps being surrounded by devout Muslims influenced me, but I found myself silently praying that I wouldn't have to return to Dohuk with Abdullah. My prayers were answered! My aunt told me that we had to leave for Kurdistan immediately—all of us—because she had received word one of her great aunts was dying. I saw the reaction in Abdullah's eyes. If I could have read a word in them it would have said, 'Damn.'

While he and Hadar were in Dohuk visiting Hadar's great aunt, I was working out ways of trying to use Abdullah to my advantage. He had a car. He was lusting after me. Car and lust. Use them, girl! I had accepted that while I remained in Kurdistan, far away from the Australian Embassy in Baghdad, escaping across the relatively close border into Turkey or Iran would be impossible without very serious help, but what still remained open to me was getting a phone call through to Ojo in Germany. Hearing his voice would be like a tonic and he would be able to do something to get me out of my predicament. I'd be able to ask him to call every Australian embassy in the world, the Australian Government—anybody he could think of. Then I'd be free and the death sentence I knew was hovering would be removed. While there was no phone in my father's house, there were two telephone exchanges—one in the city itself and the other a short drive out to the outskirts—from which international calls could be made. There was only one problem. I thought I remembered his number, but couldn't be 100 per cent sure.

I had learned about the telephone exchanges one day when I stood at the open gate—when the boys from next door were not on the roof—and got into a conversation with a girl who lived directly opposite across the narrow road. She was younger than me, but had two older sisters who I also met in time. They were warm, friendly girls, amazed that I was from Australia yet still 'one of them'. In time, our friendship grew to the point that my father would even allow me to slip across the road and visit them for brief periods.

When my father was at work, for he was employed at an engineering factory, and Hadar was with her great aunt, Abdullah dropped by at dusk with the excuse of checking that I was all right. My grandmother happened to have gone off to the shops, for she was still a sprightly woman, and perhaps Abdullah had learned I was alone somehow. But if he had any evil thoughts, I was ready for him.

'Can you do me a favour?' I asked, knowing that he would be more than willing to do anything for me if there was a sexual reward at the end.

'I'm craving for some ice-cream. Can you drive me somewhere to get some?'

We drove downtown and bought ice-creams and then I asked,

almost as an afterthought, if he wouldn't mind dropping me off quickly at one of the telephone exchanges so I could make a quick call. The exchange in the city was closed so he shrugged and said he'd have to take me to the second place, located on a hill overlooking the city.

'I'm not allowed to do this, you know,' he said. 'But I'll do it for you as a special favour. It will be our secret.' Some secret. If only he knew about mine. The exchange, as I had expected, was full of men and smoke. I had to ask Abdullah if he wouldn't mind lending me the money for the call I needed to make and he asked me not to insult him. Of course he would pay—the men would never allow a woman to pay for a phone call, although how many times would a woman be allowed to make a call anyway? I had to wait a short time before I was directed to a booth to take the call that I had asked the man at the desk to place for me. I had given him the international code for Germany—49—but I'd struggled with the rest of Ojo's number and had to give the clerk three alternatives. He was not happy about that but I begged him to help, hoping, too that Abdullah, who was sitting on a nearby bench, could not pick up my anxiety. The first two attempts failed, but on the third I heard the phone ringing.

'Tag—hello?'

It was him!

'Ojo, it's me at last! I miss you so much!'

'Hello. . . hello. . . ?'

'Ojo, can you hear me? Ojo?'

'Hello? Hello?'

I wanted to scream with frustration. I could hear him, but he couldn't hear me!

He must have known someone was trying to reach him because he kept saying hello, but then I heard the 'pip' of the phone as he hung up. His lovely voice; I'd heard it but as far as he was concerned

I hadn't called him as promised. Or perhaps he thought that was me trying to get through and might be sitting there by the phone waiting for the call to come through again.

'We have to go,' said Abdullah. 'We can't be away this long.'

Before we left, I asked one of the phone assistants why my call had failed.

'Oh, this is always a bad time to make an international call,' he said. 'It's always difficult to get through at this time. You need to wait a couple of hours.'

'Well, why didn't you tell me that?' I asked angrily, but Abdullah was already leading me away, his hand on my arm. I pushed it away. I wasn't going to let him touch me there in front of all those men in the exchange or in any other location for that matter.

As we drove back through quiet streets that were now dark he asked who I was calling. I simply told him that I hadn't got through, but he must have suspected it was an overseas call because the fee was higher than for a local connection. He put his question again in a different way, asking if I'd called a friend.

'Abdullah, just because you have made yourself very familiar with me doesn't mean that you own me or have a right to question me.'

He suddenly threw his arm up and grabbed my breast. 'Familiar like this you mean?'

I returned the compliment—by lashing out and striking him across the face. He was stunned but at least he didn't lose control of the car. Within a minute or so I saw in the street lights that his lip had swollen and there was a trickle of blood. I told him he should wipe his face or his wife would have questions to ask. How I wished I could tell her what her husband was up to but I couldn't risk destroying their relationship—and add to the dislike so many members of the family appeared to hold for me.

But I began to ask myself whether it really was dislike, or simply a demonstration of their frustration at not being able to make me one of them. If only I could reach out to someone, by phone, out there in the big wide world and just hear some reassuring words that they would get me out of my predicament, but the only number I knew was my mother's. I thought about calling her but then I remembered her final words to me that I could throw myself from a roof for all she cared, I would not be leaving Kurdistan.

From time to time I was allowed to visit my maternal grandfather's home, a cousin, Vasheen driving around to pick me up. The main reason for my visits there were to watch documentaries or the news channels—CNN and the BBC—because, unlike the televisions in my father's house, which could only pick up boring local channels, my grandfather had a satellite connection. However, even the satellite TV was censored. No entertainment, no films or music videos, just the news and documentaries. It was evening and I was watching a history channel with some of my cousins, aware that I would be taken back to my father's home shortly, when one of my uncles burst into the room and told us to quickly switch to the Al Jazeera Arab TV station.

When we flicked it on, the screen showed a tall building with smoke pouring from it. Then I saw an airplane flying towards another building and disappearing behind it. But that was just an illusion—it had slammed right into it. I was watching, with little understanding, the attack on America on the morning of 9/11.

'Those sons of whores,' my uncle cried. 'I can't believe they've done this.'

He would not have been aware of who was responsible, but he had guessed correctly that Arab terrorists had carried out the attack. Men from next door, people from the street, came to the house, one of the few in the area that had satellite TV. As the vision was replayed time and again, more people poured in through the door and the room was a crush. It didn't matter any more that I, a woman, was a stranger among men. An older sister of my mother, the aunt who had wrapped my arm in a towel when I had stabbed myself, was crying. I had come to feel sorry for her as the weeks had gone by because I learned that she had been forced into marriage at the age of 16 and then her husband had been killed in a tribal dispute and she was never allowed to marry again. Remarrying after a husband's death shows great disrespect and any widow who does it is despised.

What did these terrifying scenes mean for the Arab world? The discussion among the men in that crowded room was spot on. They predicted that George W Bush would strike back, but opinions varied on which country would be hit. They hoped it would be Iraq on the southern side of the mountains because it would mean the Americans would be doing the Kurds' work for them. It would certainly mean the end of oppression by Saddam Hussein, they all agreed, but these were wishful thoughts at that time.

When I arrived home I found that my father had already heard the news. 'As a result of this,' he said, 'there'll be another war in Iraq and I will pray every day that it will bring about the end of Saddam Hussein.' In a reference to the Gulf War which had ended in 1991 after six months, he added: 'Next time they had better make sure they get rid of Saddam. There is always the threat that he'll strike out at our people again. He's probably still got chemicals stored away somewhere.'

The events of 9/11 were on everyone's lips and yet I was still trapped in my own personal crisis. Unless America bombed Iraq and all borders opened I couldn't see any way of escaping. I had worried as each day passed that my father would tell me that a suitable cousin had been found for me to marry. My heart sank when my father asked me one morning to sit down to talk about my future. This was it, I thought. He and his relatives had found a future husband. Relief swept over me when he said he had been thinking about my education and he believed I should start a course at the University of Dohuk. I greeted the suggestion with mixed emotions—a university course would certainly get me out of the house but it would also expose me to a world of male university students who would view me as a future bride. I was now well versed in how the system worked—a man who saw a 'free' young woman at any function, usually a wedding, would send his mother around to the woman's home to ask for her hand. This was what had happened to me in Germany with Mikael. University, I learned from my occasional chats with the girls in the house across the street, was a breeding ground for marriage. I avoided my father's suggestion, telling him I'd think about what kind of course I might be interested in taking up.

My hesitation resulted in my 'grounding'. There were to be no more visits to my materal grandfather's home to watch television—they were hardly frequent events in any case—and I was once again trapped in the house. While I could venture into the garden even when the boys next door were not around, I couldn't get any exercise. It just wasn't big enough. Even hardened prisoners in the jails I'd seen in movies had far more space for recreation than I had. There was no-one to talk to during the day when my father was at work. Just my grandmother and she and I could not find a word to pass between us unless it was her asking me to clean this or wash that. Even those chores were a break from the utter boredom. In the garden I learned to recognise every lizard that ran around the wall. I knew which holes various ones lived in and I even found myself saying things like: 'Oh, there's Lizzy. Hello Lizzy.'

'You're losing your mind!' I told myself one day and that evening I informed my father that I was ready to take up a university course.

An introductory visit was arranged and with me suitably attired in a hijab and long skirt, my father and I were shown to a law professor's room. There were two other students in there, both males. They remained while my father discussed a suitable time when I might be able to start, explaining that I had received an excellent education in both Australia and Germany. There was no question that I would be enrolled but the professor needed to speak to the principal to arrange for a starting date. As we were leaving, the boys who had also been present followed us out into a corridor. One of them said that he recognised my father, but Khalid told the boy that if that was the case he couldn't recall where they had met before. The boy's eyes were all over me. I had to smile to myself: here we go again. He asked us to come for a drink in the café with him and my father agreed, but the idle chatter between him and my father over a cup of tea was just an excuse for the student, I assessed. Every few seconds his eyes would dart back to me. Right there and then I decided that university was far too dangerous for me. I was a Kurdish girl with a Western education and I was free—free in their sense but certainly not free in mine.

On the way home, I told my father I still wasn't 100 per cent sure about starting a course. I made the excuse that I felt the university course wasn't advanced enough for me and it could possibly drag me back. He seemed to understand that, but I hoped he wouldn't try to pressure me again some time.

Three days later there was a knock at the door. When my father wasn't home I was not allowed to answer anyone who came calling. I heard my grandmother call out to me to see who was there. Fine. I had permission to see who was calling. The woman who stood there was in her 40s, neatly dressed in Muslim attire and holding a box with a pink ribbon tied around it. She asked for 'the woman of the house'. I showed her to the women's room, relatively bleak as it was, but I had no right to take her into the comfortable men's room. I called for my grandmother as the visitor settled down on a cushion staring at the turned-off TV, which, when not in use, was covered with a crocheted drape. When I had first seen it I had had to stifle a laugh—the TVs had to wear a veil.

I went to my room as the two women talked for about an hour. I had found a new pastime for the hours when I was alone in the bedroom. I had learned to knit and was now busy producing a pair of baby socks for one of my pregnant aunties. I wondered what Ojo would think if he could have seen me. Would he have laughed his head off, or cried for me? I think he would have cried. Eventually my grandmother called for me and introduced me to the stranger.

'This is a relative of ours. You have met her son at the university.'

As she said this the visitor proferred the box she had brought, which I presume held sweets, the traditional greeting gift. My hands were half-way towards receiving it when my grandmother continued.

'Her son was very fond of you and he would like to ask for your hand in marriage. As your mother is not here, she has asked me to put the question to you.'

I lowered my hands. 'What do you expect me to say?' I replied. 'I don't know this lady, I've met her son for a few minutes at the university and now he wants to marry me? This is nonsense.' I turned to the visitor: 'I mean no disrespect to you but my answer is no. How can I possibly marry someone I've met for only a few minutes?'

Both women could have easily answered that by pointing out how lucky I was to have even met the boy. The first time many girls had come face to face with their husbands was when they were standing before the Imam. The disappointed mother left.

'You are not getting any younger,' my grandmother said. 'Girls are getting married at the age of 15 and as each year goes by your value is decreasing and you will end up with a less desirable husband.'

I railed on her. 'Can't you get it into your head? I am not going to be married off just because I'm an "old woman" at the age of 21. And how dare you speak of my "value" as though the only thing that matters to a man is how old his bride is. Have you ever heard of the word "love"? I doubt it. Because I certainly haven't seen any of it coming from you!'

I stormed off to my room, threw myself onto the bed and let the tears flow. That mother may have been the first to call but I knew she wouldn't be the last. There had been invitations for me to go to weddings, friends of relatives or cousins or nieces, and each time I had managed to cry off, saying that I had a headache. I would remain at home with my grandmother, her scuttling around in the kitchen and me in my room or out in the garden talking to lizards. The day would come, though, when I wouldn't be able to refuse.

Towards the end of 2001, as the winter snows turned the distant mountains white and after my birthday passed without much celebration in the house, the city came alive with news from the USA. America had launched a revenge attack on Afghanistan with the intention of destroying Osama bin Laden's training camps and removing the Taliban from power. There was jubilation all over Kurdistan for, although the attacks were against Muslim brothers, it was the Arab faction that was being hit—and the Arabs had never been kind to the Kurds. History was witness to that.

My father joined in the hope that the war against the Taliban would see them turfed out and peace return right through the region. He and the other men of the city believed that if America could put on a display of its military might in Afghanistan, the despot who was Saddam Hussein might just get off his high horse

Above: The last ever photo of me and my sister Bojeen and my mother during one of their visits to Dohuk

Above: Me with the cuddly bear given to me by Diyar, who was desperate to marry me. My right eye is still bruised from a recent beating by my father.

I wasted many hours in the front yard of my father's house—here I am wearing a dress I made and embroidered to pass the time.

This bride (second from left) was tied down and forced to have sex with her husband on their wedding night.

One day with my great aunt Fatima, I visited the tomb
of my father's tribal leader.

Top: Dohuk, showing the main highway and the mountains surrounding the city. Bottom: a typical Kurdish mountain village.

Above: Me (second from right at rear) with university students in Dohuk—a mixture of Catholics and Muslims.

Left: this photo of me and Abdulla, whose wandering hands I was always trying to avoid, was taken during Ramadan-Eid, a time of forgiving!

Top: In the centre is my supposed 'dying' grandfather. On the left is aunt Mahdia and my mother is on the right.

Above: I wore red to brighten my day when I posed for this picture with my good friends, the sisters from across the road.

Below: At a neighbour's house on the day of my father's wedding to Jamilla. I'm in the middle.

Bottom: In the men's room at the home of the sisters across the street. This is where I made my 'forbidden' phone calls.

Top: a curtain divides the men from the women at the wedding of one of my closest friends. Notice that no-one smiles. I am fifth from the left.

Above: Me and my cousin Areeman on the day I cut my hair short when I found it was falling out.

and show compassion to his people.

Khalid continued to press me to think again about university, but I had now found a legitimate reason for rejecting the notion. Almost all the classes would be in the Arabic language, which is totally different to the Kurdish, which is a mixture of Persian, Indian, some Turkish and a little Arabic. There would not be much I would be able to understand because my knowledge of Arabic was limited. However, I was improving it. Relieved that he finally saw my point of view, the ongoing problem of being asked to marry a man who might have noticed me, or heard about me, was always present. Although I managed to avoid every invitation to attend someone's wedding, the day came when my grandmother was also a guest and they were not going to leave me alone in the house. As my aunties gathered there in preparation, I put up my usual excuse of having a migraine—which was true in any case—but this time I was told: 'Take an aspirin. You're coming with us.'

The wedding of a cousin who had met her husband, another cousin, only a few times, was at the new husband's house near the centre of Dohuk. It was a typical affair with the women, and with the poor bride in her virginal white gown (I prayed for her sake that she was a virgin!), sitting in their room while the men relaxed with the groom in their more comfortable surroundings, smoking through hookahs and chatting. When it was time for food, the men, who had by now moved to a large table in the garden, were served first. They had the pick of the best parts of the meat and all the other trimmings. When they had finished, the remainder of the food was served to the women and the children.

I could feel the eyes of every man upon me in those moments when, inevitably, the two groups crossed one another, for such gatherings, I came to learn, were the true happy hunting grounds. Several men said hello, but I knew there was hidden intent behind their greetings. I tried to reassure myself that I was being silly. . . paranoid even. Surely it was reasonable for someone to glance my way or make me feel welcome.

My intuition was correct, however. The following day a woman came to the door with a small white cardboard box tied with ribbon. I didn't even need to ask who she was: the mother of one of the bachelors from the wedding, calling to ask my father or mother, or whoever was 'the woman of the house' for my hand in marriage. It was my father who received her this time and once again I shook my head. I didn't even know who her son was, let alone commit the rest of my life to him over a cardboard box of sweets.

My depression intensified. How I wished I could hear Ojo's voice, but I believed by now he had probably given up on me. I had promised to call him on my arrival in June and it was now December. He could hardly go to my mother in Germany and ask where I was. Although she had heard that I had a 'black friend'—I still recalled her spiteful words to me about him before we came to Kurdistan—she did not know who he was. In any case, Ojo, aware of my determination to keep his identity from my mother at a time when I was expecting to be settling down with Mikael, would be keeping well away from her.

Things had to change. My father knew I could not sit around moping and I was waiting for the next drama that would be cast upon me.

'I've been thinking what to do about you,' he said and once again I braced myself. Would it be another marriage proposal—one that he, not I, had agreed to?

'I've arranged with your Aunt Vian for you to work at her company,' he said. 'They have room for a secretary and I think it would be good for you. You will only be there when your aunt is there. When she goes to work, she'll pick you up and bring you back when she leaves.'

While I realised that once again this would open me up to more proposals from any unmarried man in that company, at least it would help the days to pass towards my unknown destiny. I could never have imagined the assault on my emotions or the turmoil that lay ahead.

EIGHT

My aunt worked as an engineer for a construction company. It was a converted house, with the living room used as the reception area and other rooms used as offices. There was an old bodyguard with a long grey beard sitting on a chair outside with an AK-47 gun on his lap. He smiled at us when we arrived, then took another sip of his tea from a small glass. I wondered how effective he would be if the place came under any kind of attack.

I was introduced to my immediate boss, Zana, although I was to learn in time that the owner was a relative of none other than the Kurdistan President, Massoud Barzani. Zana, in his 40s, was a stocky man with a small moustache and a very sharp brain. He had travelled on business through all the European countries and spoke reasonably good English. I wondered during our introduction, with my aunt telling me proudly of his background in his presence, what a man with so much intelligence and experience was doing working for a construction company—he should have been a high-ranking politician, I thought. But perhaps the money was good.

With my aunt happy to leave me alone with him in his office, he asked about me. It was obvious that my aunt had not told him very much, for he did not even know that I had grown up in Australia. I saw no reason to hold back the fact that my mother had brought me to Kurdistan and had left without me. I explained I wanted to leave but I had no passport and my days were being wasted just sitting around. I did not tell him about the loss of my virginity. There were only three people in the whole world who knew about that. Mikael, Ojo—and me. I had learned to trust no-one else with my secret. Even with Mikael, I feared he might start spreading the word through the Kurdish community in Germany because with me being away the threat I held against him, to reveal to the police his warehouse of stolen goods, might no longer hold good. All he had to do was get it emptied and close it down and he would hold the advantage.

As for Ojo and myself, what if he had now given up on me, believing that I had deserted him? I did not know whether he, too, might have revealed to any of his male friends how he had fallen for me and I had lied to him about going away 'for a short holiday'. Would he have told them that I'd be in trouble if I went off with another man? Would that gossip have spread through the Kurdish community in Germany? All these thoughts had haunted me as the weeks went by and now I had come face to face with another man, my new boss, who was asking questions, innocent though they were, about my previous life. Would he tell his bachelor friends about my 'availability'? So many questions, each one enhancing my fear.

The office work I was given was easy enough and although there was a computer—I had learned to use one in Germany—it was old, with a dark screen and a flashing green cursor. My first thought when I saw it was that I'd be able to send out SOS emails to every friend whose address I could remember. That hope was quickly dashed. There was no internet connection; the computer was good only for typing up documents and printing them. Every dream vanished as quickly as it came.

I fell into a comfortable routine, travelling in with my aunt each day, returning with her towards the end of the afternoon. At least I wasn't sitting around with my grandmother.

A new project was in the pipeline—literally. The company was invited to join with others in Dohuk in expressing an interest in building an ambitious $US2 million water pipe that would run from a lake in Syria to the poor villages of Kurdistan. The scheme was being run under the control of the United Nations, which had an office in Dohuk. Zana asked if I would attend a meeting that had been arranged for all the interested construction companies. As I could speak Kurdish and English, I would be perfect as an interpreter for the British UN representative who was holding the meeting in the UN compound.

Fifteen representatives from the interested companies gathered in a board room with a large round table in the compound. The UN representative, who I will call David, had been with the organisation for a number of years, travelling throughout the Middle East. Even as I set about interpreting for Zana and my aunt, who were both present, my mind was racing. This handsome man, aged in his early 40s I estimated, was from London. If I had the opportunity to explain my plight to him he would surely understand and try to do something to help me. He worked for the UN, after all. I began to assure myself that they would have to help. Although formalities were the order of the day, I managed to speak to him afterwards, with my aunt standing close by, for she wasn't going to allow any informal discussion. Even so, aware that he was a foreigner talking privately to a 'local woman', we managed a few words. In fact, it was he who approached me and asked where I was from because my knowledge of English had impressed him. When I told him I was from Australia 'originally'—that word was for the benefit of my aunt, if she happened to overhear—he seemed surprised that I should now be here in a small place like Dohuk.

'Look, why don't you and your aunt come for some tea with me at the Jyan,' he suggested, referring to the biggest and best hotel in Dohuk.

'I'll ask her,' I said. But I already knew what the answer would be.

'No. Now is not the time,' she said.

I told David that we had to get back to work to start working on the outline plans he had asked all the company representatives to submit. He handed his business card to each of us, but made sure that everyone else in the room received one too. He gave me a look as he handed me his card and I could feel him watching as I left the room.

The following day, when I answered the phone at the office, I recognised his voice immediately. He didn't identify himself, asking to speak to Zana. When I said he wasn't available, David said: 'Perhaps just as well because I really wanted to say hello to you.'

I thanked him for the compliment. He went on to confirm what I expected, that it had been a relief for him to be able to speak to a woman whose natural tongue was English. But I also picked up that it was more than our shared language that had provoked his call. He didn't say so directly, but I suspected he would like to meet me again. He would have known, as I did, that the likelihood of that was just about zero.

A few days later, he called again, asking for Zana, but telling me before I put him through that he had arranged for our company, along with others, to visit a site where the pipeline would be laid. The proposals that the various companies could put forward after visiting the site, would lead to him picking one of them for the work.

'Make sure you come as the interpreter,' he urged.

Although it was now the spring of 2002, it was on a bleak, windy and chilly landscape that we gathered to look at the area where the proposed pipeline would run. Rugged up against the weather, my aunt, Zana and I, along with the two other company representatives, were greeted by David before we began wandering around over stones and sand. I pretended for my aunt's and Zana's benefits to be focused on the discussions but I was once again thinking about how I could ask David to help me. Apart from that, I found it such a relief to be able to chat to someone in English.

He wasn't going to miss an opportunity either and extended another invitation for me, my aunt and Zana to join him for lunch at the hotel. This time, with Zana present, my aunt agreed it would be all right. In the dining room, David arranged it so that he would be sitting next to me and we would be able to slip in the occasional conversation about Australia. He mentioned that he was 'Down Under' just a year ago and was looking forward to the time he could return. How I wished I could jump on the same plane with him!

I couldn't help it—I felt tears well up. I hoped my aunt and Zana didn't notice, but David did. He shot me an anxious glance but did not say anything. In order to break my mood, he asked Zana about the company, how long it had been in operation and as I had to interpret his question and the answer I was able to remove myself quickly from thoughts of Australia to where I was at this business lunch. Or perhaps I should say the 'fake' business lunch, for I was convinced that David had arranged it so he and I could chat a little more.

The next time he called, it was as though I was expecting his next words.

'Latifa, is there any chance we could meet away from your aunt and your boss. . . Just you and me for a short time?'

My heart leaped. I hadn't been able to get him out of my mind. Not only did I like him, feel some affinity to him given our backgrounds, but I also believed he could be the one person who could help me leave Kurdistan.

'How can I possibly meet you? I can't get away from here. I can't get away from my father's house, either. And you definitely cannot come to me.' I was almost inclined to add the jokey remark that he didn't even have a mother to send around to me, but I immediately told myself that there was nothing amusing about my plight.

'I could get one of my drivers to pick you up and perhaps you could tell Zana that there were some papers that I wanted to give him in relation to the pipe project. Do you think that would work?'

I thought about it. It would only work if my aunt was absent. Zana would probably agree to it because he would think the company was getting close to winning the project.

'I won't be able to stay long in your office,' I told David. 'It will have to look as though I'm just picking up documents—and please have something ready for me or everyone here will be suspicious.'

'Uhh, Latifa, you cannot come to the office. There are too many people around here who would talk. They might think that you have come to pay me a bribe, anything like that. It's too much of a risk for you and for me. Will you come to my house, which is near the compound? It will be far safer for both of us. My driver can be trusted.'

I was told what to do. At midday the following day, when I knew my aunt would be in another part of the city, and having obtained Zana's approval, I was picked up by David's driver in a white UN car with the initials in blue on the side. Zana came to the door and watched as I got in. He must have been impressed, particularly as he thought I was going to pick up some paperwork for him regarding the pipeline project.

David's house was a large white two-storey building with a UN flag flying over the front gate and another on the roof. As instructed, I did not go in through the front entrance but was directed by the driver to a way in through the kitchen at the rear. If anyone saw me going in, they would hopefully think that I was one of the kitchen staff. An Assyrian housekeeper, as usual without a *hijab* for they are Catholics, was busy in the kitchen and nodded a greeting towards me. There would be no chance of gossip by her, for the Assyrians were far more 'Westernised'.

David was waiting for me, dressed casually in an open-neck white shirt. He invited me to sit on a sofa and asked if I would like coffee. He apologised that it was only Nescafe. Only Nescafe! I hadn't seen or tasted it since leaving Germany and I welcomed the offer. He sat opposite me as we danced around with words, discovering that we had exactly the same birthday. If that was not an omen, I did not know what was. Then I brought the subject around to explaining how much I wanted to return to Australia but there was no-one who could help me because I did not even have a passport. I told him, however, that I had all my passport details written on that piece of paper.

'I'll do what I can to help you, Latifa,' he said. 'I'm sure I'll be able to do something to get you out of here.'

I wondered if I had told him enough to convince him of the urgency for me to leave. Dare I tell him the real reason—that I was not a virgin and that would bring about my death, like it had so many other young women?

Without further thought, I began telling him.

'David, you must keep this to yourself but there is a very strong reason why I must leave,' I began.

He sat back in his chair without comment, waiting for me to go on.

'You see, I am not a virgin. It happened in Germany. A passionate moment turned into a rape. I didn't want it to happen but the fact is, it did.'

He brought a closed hand to his face, his forefinger against his cheekbone, absorbed in my 'confession'.

'I see,' he said. Then he sat in silence for a short while, just staring at me. I felt compelled to tell him that it was my very own cousin who had raped me, but I stopped myself. Surely he did not need to know any more.

Finally he said: 'You are indeed in a very dangerous situation. It hasn't escaped me how eligible you are. You must have had every man in town after you. It can only be a matter of time before your father lines you up with someone.'

'And that will be the end of me.'

I told him about my cousin who had been driven out into the desert and killed. I also relayed to him the story I had heard in Germany of a Kurdish woman called Pele, living in Sweden, who had campaigned against honour killings. She began a relationship with a Swedish man and when she returned to Dohuk in 1999 for a holiday, she was shot dead by her uncle because he believed she had brought shame to the family.

He shook his head. 'No, Latifa, I won't let that happen to you. I'll do everything in my power to get you away. That's a promise.'

I wanted to leap up and throw myself on him and hug him and thank him, for he was the first person who had said anything like that. There was an infectious charm about him and I felt I could trust him. He was the UN, for heaven's sake. If I couldn't trust him, then who could I trust?

I had to leave. I already feared I had been away too long. He gave me some documents to take back with me concerning the pipeline project—a more detailed map of the area where the project would start and it would be enough to give to Zana—and when we stood, he gave me a peck on the cheek. He took my hand and I took his. I looked deep into his eyes and thought: 'Don't betray me, David. Don't betray me like the others.'

I managed to go to his house three more times over the following weeks on the pretext of picking up more plans for the pipe project and our personal relationship blossomed, so that each time I left him we embraced with a passionate kiss, but it went no further than that. Each time I was with him, I forgot all about my troubles. I enjoyed his company, his touch, so much and I knew that I was falling for him. But while I believed our burgeoning relationship was a secret between us—and when I say relationship, I'm talking about a total of three snatched hours at that stage!—Zana, smart, intelligent, watchful Zana, had already seen how attracted David was to me. There had been that initial meeting in the UN board room, the visit to the pipeline site, the lunch. Then there were my trips to pick up more documents. Zana read through the bluff perfectly.

One day he called me into his office and closed the door.

'Latifa, I want to talk to you about David,' he said. I felt a lump come to my throat. He knew! He knew what I'd been up to. But what he said came as such a shock that I remained speechless.

'I want you to work on a mission for us,' he said. I correctly assumed that 'us' meant he and the owner. 'I know what's going on with you and him and I think you can be of assistance to us.'

'What do you mean?'

His eyes met mine as he sat back in his chair, slouching in a way that his stomach stuck out, and he lit up a cigarette. He appeared to be composing his words before he finally spoke.

'I want you to secretly get some important information from the UN for us,' he said.

I couldn't believe what I was hearing. It had to be some kind of joke. I didn't reply. I just sat staring at him.

'You are probably aware of your mother's work for us,' he continued. 'She has been a faithful servant for Kurdistan. She had all the attributes and you, of course, are your mother's daughter. Men are falling over you—don't worry, I've seen it—you speak English, you speak Kurdish and you are intelligent.'

There was that phrase again—'your mother's daughter.' It had been used against me by my grandmother and now it was being used—favourably?—to encourage me to be. . . a spy?

'As you know, Latifa, we have struggled for decades for our independence here in Kurdistan, to be totally free of the dangerous regime of Saddam Hussein. Along the way, our people have been murdered and at the very least persecuted. Our towns and villages have been ransacked and you will know about the gassing of hundreds of our people just a few years ago. We are supposed to receive protection and aid from the UN—and you know better than anyone that they are represented here.'

He gave me a long look as he said that. Had I been followed to David's home? His stare sent a wave of unease through my body.

'At every opportunity our people are leaving, looking for a new life in the West because they fear that Saddam Hussein has not finished yet.'

People might be leaving, I thought, but not me. I had no documents. I was a nobody.

I finally found my tongue. I had hardly taken in what he had been saying aside from a few words. . . spy. . . people leaving. . .

'You want me to be a spy?'

He slowly nodded.

'Are you crazy? What do I know about spying? And who do you want me to spy on?' Although even as I asked the question I knew what his answer was going to be.

He exhaled and watched the smoke rise.

'David,' he said.

'You're crazy. I'm not going to spy on anyone.' Particularly David, I thought. He was my ticket out of this cursed place.

'If you do this for us,' he said, 'I promise I will help you to go home.'

Another promise! Another offer of help to leave. Who was I to believe?

He read the disbelief on my face. 'There are people I know who have only to snap their fingers and all the doors will be opened for you. But they won't do it unless you give something in return.'

'Zana,' I said. 'All I've heard in the past months are lies. I've been betrayed by my own mother, I've been physically abused by my own father, I've had men leering at me like sex-hungry dogs and I've been locked up like a prisoner. I don't belong here. I might be a child of Kurdistan but I'm also an Australian. My home is Sydney, not Dohuk. You have no claim on me to work for you or your government.'

He was silent for a moment. 'We are your only way out,' he said at last.

But David had promised to help me, too. Yet I was being asked to spy on him. Whose side should I take? Whose promises of help were real?

'What are you asking me to do?'

Zana stood and began pacing his office. 'We want you to find out what the UN's relationship is with Iraq, with Saddam Hussein.'

'Are you crazy! This is deadly serious stuff. This is high-powered politics!'

'Relax. We simply want you to find out what projects the UN is negotiating with the Iraqi Government. They are helping us, but we believe they are also helping Saddam Hussein. How are they helping him? What support are they giving him? It's vitally important to know everything about the relationship between Saddam and the UN. We have others working to this end, but you have, what shall I say, an advantage.'

'I still don't understand what this is all about.'

He slumped back into his chair. 'If the UN is involved with Iraq in, say, a project like the very one you and I have been negotiating— the pipeline—we need to know about it.'

'I see—so you can blow it up and then it will turn his army onto the Kurdish people and they'll all get gassed again.' The sarcasm in my voice shocked me and startled him.

'Will you do it?'

'Do what? I still don't know what you're asking me to do.'

He smiled. 'Get close to this man David. Read his documents. Find out who they are from. Find out who he is in contact with. That's all we need to know.'

'I won't do it. I'm not a spy, for God's sake. I've been betrayed by others and I won't. . . .'

I stopped myself, but he finished the sentence for me. 'Betray him? How can you betray someone you hardly know, Latifa?'

It was a good point. I had thrown myself onto David at the beginning because I believed he could help me escape and then I had begun to have feelings for him. But I didn't really know him. Even so, I was not going to spy on him. I wasn't going to spy on anybody.

'I'm sorry, Zana. You can sack me from this job for all I care. I won't do it.'

'Think about it overnight. You know me. You don't really know him. I'm offering you the chance of leaving Kurdistan if you just do this small job for us.'

That night I couldn't sleep. Zana had virtually confirmed my earlier thoughts that my mother was a spy. She had all the attributes. Yes, Baian was attractive, she could speak English, Kurdish, Arabic and German.

She was, in fact, the perfect spy.

Now they wanted me to take up her work, not on the same large scale, but work as a spy nonetheless. Could I really betray David after he had promised to help me? Who should I place my trust in—him or Zana? Two offers of help to get out of this place. If I made the wrong choice who knew if the chance would ever arise again?

I sat up in my bed and put on the light. It was close to three o'clock in the morning. My eyes went around the room, to all the furniture my mother and father had acquired when they were young. It was dark and heavy, custom made from hard wood. Even the mattress had been theirs—similar to a Japanese futon, packed so tight with lamb's wool that there was no 'give' in it and it had taken me some time to become accustomed to it after the soft mattresses of Australia and Germany. I wanted no part of their life, as it had been then, or now. I just wanted out.

I remembered a phrase from a book I had once read about espionage in the Soviet Union during the Cold War. How British spies had been lured into giving away secrets by beautiful women working for the KGB. Zana wanted me to play the same role against David. He called it a mission for Kurdistan, but I knew it by another name.

A honey trap.

NINE

My grandmother kept chickens in a cage in the back garden. There was also a rooster, which roamed free. She wouldn't allow the rooster and the chickens to get together because she was coy about sex, according to my aunt in Baghdad. It was the rooster's crowing that woke me a few hours later, along with the honk, honk, of a donkey some people along the street kept.

I stared at the concrete ceiling, etched into which was a floral pattern, the only concession to anything vaguely attractive in that grim room. From the ceiling hung a fake chandelier, powered by electricity, which would fail every three hours at indeterminate times. If it happened during the day, my grandmother and I would have to wait for my father to come home from work so he could use his strength to pull the cord and start our small generator.

It was with a heavy heart that I made my way out to the lounge to eat breakfast. I had made up my mind what I was going to tell

Zana. I just prayed it was the right decision.

My aunt collected me as usual, stopping by the house in the company's car. On the way to the office my whole body was trembling. Zana's words from the previous day swept through my mind. He could even get me out without a passport, he had said. Mixed with this memory were words my father had used many years previously in Australia: 'Always remember, Latifa, to treat people as you would wish to be treated yourself.' Time and again those words had returned to me throughout the early part of that morning, warning me against spying on David as I had asked myself whether I was beginning to fall in love with him, or fall for him because I'd seen him as some kind of saviour.

I was trapped in a kind of mental no man's land, between betrayal of, and infatuation for, the man from the United Nations. Had my mother been as confused as me when she had been 'approached'? I still had no absolute proof that she had been involved in espionage— just Zana's suggestion of it and her mysterious behaviour, flying to and from London, making numerous trips to Kurdistan and clearly holding sway with men in high places. She had been playing a dangerous game and now I had been asked by Zana, whose company I had decided was merely a front for more sinister activities, to take similar risks.

'I'll do it,' I said when I entered his office. 'But I'll only do it on one condition. That you will give me your word you will do everything in your power to get me out of Kurdistan when I've done what you want me to do.'

'Of course I'll do that,' he said. 'You have my word.'

'So what do I do?'

'Give me a day or two and I'll let you know.'

I hardly remember much of the rest of the day. My emotions rose and fell. Which was more important for me—betraying someone or escaping from Kurdistan? Selfishness won that mental argument. I knew I would lose my mind if I remained there for much longer. Or lose my life.

The following day was Friday. Mosque day. Everything was closed, like Sundays in the West—or rather like Sundays used to be. I spent the day dreaming of what I would do when I was free. In the closet where I kept my clothes was a drawer with a key—a key that I'd found in the lock when I had first arrived and which I'd hidden to prevent those nosey aunties of mind probing through the few things that I held precious.

There was a small diary in which I'd scribbled some of my thoughts since I'd arrived, as well as some drawings of houses and trees that my little sister had sketched and given to me when we were still in Germany. As part of my daily idlings, I had sketched things around the house—a section of wall, a corner of the building, a copy of the design on the carpet. These images depicted my cloistered world. How I wished I could stroll down the street and sit sketching the scenes—the men in their track-suit-like clothing or kaftans walking by; the various styles of the women, the Muslims in their *hijabs* and long dresses right down to the ankles and the Assyrians in their more Western attire; the donkeys, the scooters, the children rolling hoops through the laneways. But, as always, it was not allowed. A young woman who lived next door had given me a fashion magazine to read—brought to her from a friend visiting from Europe. She asked if I could keep it for her because her family would be furious if they found it. There was something even more dangerous she asked me to look after for her: a CD of a sexually explicit movie. There was nowhere in her house where she could either watch it or keep it, but I said I'd be able to hide it for her. So it went into my 'secret drawer'. Heaven help me if any of my relatives were able to open it and one of my male cousins who had a CD player put the disc on.

I had by now made good friends with the group of four sisters living directly across the street—girls my father and grandmother allowed me to visit from time to time, as long as I quickly dashed across the narrow roadway, which was really little more than a lane. All houses in the street were crammed together, with families virtually living on top of one another. The youngest of the sisters was 16 and the oldest was 24, a sad woman because she wanted to get married but so far nobody had asked her because, truth be told, she did not have the beauty that men craved. She was olive skinned and the lighter your colour, the greater your chances at marriage. In contrast to Western tradition, the chubbier a girl is, the more suitable she is in the eyes of a suitor. This woman had given up school early, too, in order to train as a good housewife but the offers of marriage had failed to come in. Shilan, the sister I was closest to was the third oldest, two years younger than me, and she had the purest outlook on life—she never criticised anyone and gave the impression of being utterly honest.

I tried to visit them whenever their parents were out, when we could talk freely. They enjoyed listening to me telling them about Australia, about kangaroos and koalas and animals they had only seen in picture books. Like me when I was in my late teens, Shilan it turned out, knew absolutely nothing about sex, except having the general knowledge that after a girl was married she began to have children. I began to teach her about the birds and the bees, much to her astonishment and amusement, and how important it was for her to be absolutely certain she did not allow any man to touch her before she was married. I did not tell her what had happened to me.

The sisters had a satellite dish TV and when their parents were away they would flick through channels looking for any kind of Western music. Even though such entertainment channels were blocked, sometimes music could be found and they would be totally engrossed in it. They had asked their parents for permission to search out music channels but had been told in the strictest manner that such things were 'the work of the devil'.

It was the same with my father. When he reminded me that my 22nd birthday was coming up at the end of that year of 2002, he asked me what I would like. Surprised, I said: 'Getting a satellite TV link would be nice, so I could watch educational channels.'

He saw through that one. He knew that the more I watched European channels the harder it would be to draw me into the Muslim world that he, and more particularly my mother, wanted me to be part of. Watching such programs would only increase my hankering to return to Australia, he correctly assumed.

In my occasional 'trips' across the road to the girls' home I made it clear to them that I was trying to return to Europe or Australia. The oldest girl, the one who was still praying for a husband, repeated to me what was general knowledge: the only way to escape was to get married and pray that the husband was prepared to leave Kurdistan with you. If he wanted to stay, then you had to stay too.

On that Friday, the day after telling Zana I would do his spying work and while my father was at the mosque, I slipped across the street to the girls' house and knocked on the door. My friend Shilan answered.

'Is your father at home?' I asked. It was our code for my telling her I would like to use their phone. I'd used it a few times to call David for a minute or so.

'Are you going to speak English again?' she asked, knowing that even that was shameful among Kurds in Dohuk unless it was absolutely necessary to use the language to converse with a foreigner. She could not understand what I was saying on the phone but she loved to listen to the language and, while feeling a little odd about having a listener nearby at first, I soon became accustomed to her sitting in. My excuse to her, in case she accidentally let slip about my phone calls, was that I was speaking to a Kurdish-American man about work.

Their telephone, an old red 'brick' with square white push-button numbers was in the men's room, so I had to ensure that not only was the girls' father away, but also their two brothers. We all entered the men's room and the sisters sat around me in a semi-circle to watch me, in my Arabian gown, ring David. They loved these moments, finding great excitement among themselves when they recognised a word or two like 'okay' or 'coffee'. We had an agreement that if any of the men returned unexpectedly and found us in their room I would pretend to have called by to borrow one of the books that were kept there.

My heart beat faster when I heard David's voice. How wonderful it was to feel all my troubles fall away each time I heard him, for he had such a soft English accent.

'I was just thinking of you, Latifa,' he said, 'but of course I can't just pick up the phone and call you because you don't have a telephone at home.' He still called me at the office because I was the one who answered the phones, but I had to be very careful that no-one overheard me speaking English.

'What were you thinking about?'

'Oh, your beautiful smile,' he said. 'All the time I just see your smile. I'd like to see you again, if we can arrange it somehow.'

'Me too, David. And have you had any further thoughts about how I can leave here?'

I was praying that he would say yes, that he'd contacted the Australian embassy and things were in hand for my rescue.

'I'm still working on that,' he said

'All I would ask is that you tell me immediately if you aren't going to be able to help.'

When I returned to my father's house I was in an emotional turmol, playing mind games with myself, trying to guess the answers. Is he going to help you? Yes. Are you absolutely sure? No. Are you falling in love with him? Yes. Are you absolutely sure? Yes. Are you really going to spy on him? Probably.

The company car with my aunt arrived shortly before 8.30 the following morning after I had taken my usual breakfast pickings of eggs from the chickens out the back, some salty cheese, bread and tahini paste. As usual, I had sat with my father and his mother, who had not said a word of greeting to me as if it was just too much trouble for her. These days when we sat on the floor around the breakfast tray I sat with legs crossed and my back perfectly straight, reaching forward with a straight back to pick up the food. I had not forgotten my father's 'lesson' months before on how I should sit. There had been a family gathering for lunch in the first weeks of my arrival and I had been wearing a loosely fitting top. As I leaned forward to take some food, my father, noticing part of my cleavage, jumped up, walked around to me, grabbed my hair and yanked my head back.

'Never sit like that again,' he whispered, loud enough for all to hear. 'Watch how your aunts are sitting and learn!'

My grandmother's lips were tight at that moment. I wondered if she were stifling a smile or just simply expressing her disapproval at my lack of respect. From the time I first started work at the company, my father would check me over to ensure that I was dressed 'appropriately'. I was allowed to wear a pair of jeans I had been permitted to keep, although that was rather pointless because I had to wear the long kaftan-style robes over them to hide the shape of my behind. If he felt I was not dressed according to his wishes, he would insist I changed into something else before he would allow me to go to the office. Sometimes, in order not to increase his displeasure, I would wear the headscarf, with my long hair tucked up underneath, with only a fringe showing and the rest of the scarf would be thrown back loosely over my shoulder. I certainly wasn't going to wear it pulled tightly around my face, like many of the women. I was also brazen in that I dared to reveal my toes in my open-toed court shoes! I had to meet most of my father's wishes or he would put a stop to my office work and then it would be impossible to contact David. Even Zana would have no say over the wishes of my father.

Every day, Khalid was working at turning me into a modest Muslim woman and each time, while I complied with his dress requirements, I fought him mentally. I was not going to allow him, or his mother or his sisters to beat me down with their rules and how they thought I should behave. If I did not fight them, my defences would fall and the next minute I might find myself standing with a husband in front of the Imam. I felt like I was in a kind of Catch-22. In order to win my freedom, I had to make myself a prisoner.

My aunt was equally modestly dressed on this particular morning, showing no flesh at all except her hands and her face. And very little colour in her clothing. Red, in particular, was banned from everyday clothing. It was, they had made clear to me, a colour that only 'tarts' wore. Red lipstick was also a no-no. Jewellery was approved of, as long as it was worn in a modest amount. Surprisingly, my mother had sent me some gold bangles and while at first I was shocked by this act of kindness—was she feeling guilty at last?—I realised the true intent. She knew that I preferred silver to gold, but all the women in Kurdistan wore gold. This, I was convinced, was another move to pull me into the culture, removing me further from all that I had loved in the West. She would send more gold pieces as the months went by and my earlier suspicions turned into convictions. What was also bizarre was that there was never a letter with these gifts, not even a note. Just my name on the outside of the package. Nothing about my little sister, who she knew I loved, or about my brother's progress with his studies. The most recent package carried a telling message. . .

In Australia and Germany she had always bought me a nice leather diary for each coming year. This time a diary had arrived. But it wasn't just for the coming year of 2003, but also for 2004. It was obvious to me that she expected me to be still in Kurdistan for at least the next two years. I could almost hear her mocking me 'You're stuck there girl. Get used to it'.

When I arrived at the office on that Saturday morning I could see Zana through the glass window of his office chatting away with one of President Barzani's relatives, who was a joint owner of the company. My aunt went to her office and I to mine. A pile of paperwork had been left for me with a note on the top instructing what was required of me. The office tea 'boy', Saigvan, who was in his late teens brought in my tea as usual with its three lumps of sugar in the small glass, and spent a few minutes grumbling about various things, including the old guard on the front gate. I took the opportunity during these brief encounters to give him five words of English to learn each day. This time I was simply going through the motions, waiting to be called to Zana's office, a call that I knew would surely come.

Finally, when my aunt had received her instructions from him and had set off from the office to one of the city's building sites, Zana put his head around the door and beckoned me to follow. The Barzani relative had left his office. We sat opposite one another across his desk.

'So, Latifa, two days have passed,' he said. 'Is your answer still the same? You'll do this work?'

While I had told him—and myself—previously that I would, a

flash of doubt hit me.

'Zana, I've been badly betrayed more than once in recent years and I wouldn't be able to face another let-down. If I do this work for you, can you promise me that you will help me leave?'

'I've given you my word, haven't I? And I would have hoped that, even without this reward that you are asking, you would be happy to help the country of your birth, just as your mother has.'

'I would not be doing it just because my mother did it,' I said, trying to control the anger in my voice. 'I will do anything to help the Kurdish people without needing to follow in my mother's footsteps. Particularly the women. If anything I do will help them get some kind of freedom, even in the smallest way, I'll do whatever you ask. But yes, I do seek a reward. It's not money, it's not houses—just your help in getting me out of here.'

He nodded in agreement. 'In good time, you'll be on your way. Only you, Latifa, can do this—find out what the UN is up to because we believe they are heavily involved with the Saddam regime in some way. Any names you can give us, any plans, any documents, we want to see them. At the end of the day, Latifa, indirectly, you will be helping girls like yourself. We need to overthrow Saddam because in doing so, doors will be open. Curfews will be lifted, goods will flow in through the whole of Iraq. Just imagine it.'

'I can imagine it,' I said, 'but I'm dealing in reality. I need to get out. How can you assure me that you will keep your promise?'

'Wait.'

He left the office and returned with the Koran. He placed it on his desk and put his hand on it.

'On this Holy Book and the word of God, I swear I will not break the promise I have made to you, Latifa.'

I was convinced. I heard enough stories about the terrible fate that had befallen those who had broken promises made on the

Koran, or who had defiled it. They had been blinded, wounded, lost their minds. My parents had once told me of a Turkish woman entertainer who used to dance on the Koran as part of her act— before an earthquake split the building in half and even split the Koran right through the middle. It sounded apocryphal but, at my young age, the story made a big impression on me.

'Your aunt must not know about our arrangement,' said Zana. 'Tomorrow we will start to make preparations.'

'What preparations?'

'Tomorrow, you will be brought to the office as usual. Your aunt will be away on an inspection and we can start to prepare you.'

I tried to act normally when I got home that evening. I did not want my father or my grandmother to notice any change in me although my heart was pounding with both excitement and fear. What had Zana meant when he spoke of preparing me? I dreamed up a scenario of lying in bed with David and asking him what kind of work he did for the UN. I also saw myself in my imaginings, creeping out of bed and rifling through his briefcase. Was that what Zana was going to encourage me to do? But no, of course not, I assured myself. Such scenarios suggested that he knew I was not a virgin, or was at least prepared to sacrifice my virginity, my reputation and possibly my life in exchange for my freedom.

On my arrival at the office the following day and after my aunt had been despatched on her latest round of building site inspections, Zana led me out to his flatbed four-wheel drive, with the name Toyota across the back. Everyone drove one in Dohuk because they were sturdy vehicles for tackling the stony tracks to mountain villages or negotiating slippery roads when the snows fell.

We headed north east, towards the mountains that separated Kurdish Iraq from Kurdish Turkey, turning off the road onto a dusty track just short of the small town of Zawita. He then stopped and told me to change places with him and get into the driving seat. I told him I couldn't drive. That was why I was here, he said. To learn.

'You are going to need to know how to drive—just in case.'

'In case of what?'

'In case of anything at all. It's better to know how to drive than not to know.'

I told him that I knew that no woman was allowed to drive in Kurdistan but he insisted that it would be to my benefit to learn. And so my lesson began. He explained the principles to me, what the foot pedals were for, how the gears worked and how to change them. Then, with a wide open space of packed hard desert sand in front of me, I started up the car and jerked forward in first gear, the vehicle leaping like a bucking hare and swerving in all directions. No wonder he chose such a wide learning ground. Now and again he would slap my leg and shout 'Clutch!' or grab my hand and drag it onto the gearstick to change gear. For once I had no impression that his grabs at me were of a sexual nature. I knew that Zana was married and that his wife was in Europe—another spy?—but I felt no threat from him.

But for every mistake I made, he would punch my arm and yell 'No, no, no!' His instructions were driven brutally and at one stage I hit back at him, striking him in the face.

'I've had enough of this shit!' I cried. 'You're hurting me every time you slap me. I bruise easily. Just stop hitting me.'

But ignoring the pain I must have inflicted when I hit him, he just said: 'Do it! Keep going. Don't give up. This is not just for me, Latifa. This is for you, too.'

He led me through all the stages of driving—speeding forward, breaking without skidding, reversing. Once or twice he reached over and took my chin in his hands and twisted my head towards the rear, vision mirror. 'See that mirror. It's not to look in to see what you look like. It's to see what's behind you. Use it! Use it every 10 seconds or so. Always be aware of who's behind you.'

In between sips of water and a snack he had brought for us, I persevered. I learned how to drive extremely slowly, in first gear, without stalling and even managed one successful handbrake turn at speed like you see in the movies with the vehicle spinning its rear around to face the opposite direction and ready to race off again. What a sight it must have been had anyone been watching—a woman in a kaftan spinning and weaving around the desert with an angry man beside her. But by the end of the day I felt quite confident behind the wheel. I even managed to imagine myself sweeping along a freeway in Australia, heading towards Sydney.

We arrived back at the office after lunch, Zana at the wheel to take us back into town. He needed no excuse for being away with me. He told other staff members that we had been out looking at building sites and certainly the dusty state of his car bore testimony to that.

If I thought my driving lessons were over, I was mistaken. The following day, it was the same routine. My aunt was despatched to a further round of inspections while I was despatched to the desert again. Zana said if I did well this time we would not need to return.

'I thought you said I did well enough yesterday,' I said.

'You aren't going to be driving across wide open spaces every day, if it ever comes to you having to use a car. And remember it may not even occur. These lessons are just a backup. Today we'll be following along a track. Get used to it, treat it like a track and treat it like a city road.'

So I learned how to keep to the right and how to signal in advance of a turn. I knew that such manoeuvres took days or even weeks in

Australia, but I had acquired the basics in just two days.

After a lunch snack, Zana said there was one more lesson. He ordered me into the driving seat and to start the ignition. Next he told me to drive slowly enough for him to be able to walk beside the car. That was easy enough. I was now proficient at driving at a snail's pace. I stared ahead at the vast desert, the mid-summer heat creating illusions of expanses of water; the mirages that I had read about in novels.

Suddenly a loud crack that made my eardrums ring exploded beside me. I jammed my foot on the brake. The car stalled because I had not used the clutch. I swung my head around in great alarm to Zana. He was standing there with a pistol that he had fired into the air.

'That, Latifa, is what I mean about driving under distraction. Imagine a situation where someone is firing at you and you have to drive away. What are you going to do. Stall the car so they can run up and shoot you in the head?'

'What are you talking about!' I screamed. 'What are you getting me in to? I'm never going to be in a position where people are going to be shooting at me, for God's sake. Take me home, Zana. Take me home this instant!'

He shook his head. 'No-one's going to be shooting at you. What you'll be doing won't be dangerous like that. But the day might come when you'll thank me for this. Regard these lessons as backup. Nothing else. An advantage you'll have over every woman in Kurdistan and over very many men.'

So I persevered, driving slowly while he walked beside me occasionally firing his pistol. How strange the body reacts. Even though I was expecting more gunshots, when the first few came I still managed to jam my foot on the brake and stall. But after an hour, and who knew how many bullets, I was confident enough not to be put off by the gunshots. In fact, I learned to accelerate and swerve around stone markers he had placed on the desert track whenever the pistol went off. If I was fired at in a dangerous situation I would at least have a chance of making a break for it—but I was determined I would never be in such a position.

As we headed back to Dohuk I questioned Zana about my 'mission' involving David. My driving lessons appeared to have nothing to do with reading paperwork that David had.

'As I said, Latifa, it's better to have those skills than not.'

He emphasised how important it was for the Kurdish authorities to know what projects the UN was involved in with Saddam's government. He still did not explain just why it was so important but I surmised that if the Kurds found out that Saddam was involved in, for example, getting a pipeline built, it would make a good target for Kurdish extremists.

'Before you start working on your friend David, there are still more things you need to learn,' he said. 'Your initiative must also be tested.'

After the pressures of the desert—although I actually enjoyed being out in the open like that—returning to my father's home was a relief, although I had never believed I could have thought that.

There were other things I had to learn. My initiative had to be tested. I wondered what Zana had meant by that.

TEN

The Taliban had been pushed out of Kabul by the Northern Alliance and allied forces led by the Americans. The Americans and the British had carried out bombing raids in the mountains bordering Pakistan but there had been no indication that Osama bin Laden had been killed. Now, in that summer of 2002, George W Bush was accusing Saddam Hussein of destroying files relating to weapons of mass destruction and taking steps to bluff international teams preparing to go to Iraq to look for evidence of such weapons.

The belief in Kurdistan was that the Americans were going to hit Iraq, whether there was evidence of weapons of mass destruction or not. How ironic that I, who had never had any interest in wars—they were always events that happened a long way away—found myself praying that conflict would come to Iraq, but not Kurdistan as that would be too dangerous, because that might provide me with an added avenue of escape, if all else had failed. . . meaning David or Zana. There would be foreign troops everywhere, refugees would be crossing borders without documents—and I could join them. But that was wishful thinking.

While the Kurds wanted to see Saddam overthrown and welcomed American action, the Imams in the mosques were also preaching war, not peace, in their sermons. I knew this, and so did all the women in the street where I lived because of the proximity of the local mosque.

When my father was at the mosque saying his prayers and listening to the Imam after his call to prayer on Fridays, I would sit with the girls across the road listening to his voice being unintentionally carried out by loudspeaker across the immediate neighbourhood. He would speak about the power of men over women and he would ask for ongoing prayers for the freedom-fighting PDK (Party Democratic of Kurdistan). Men had power and politics was power, I'd hear him say. Every man had to pray that the PDK would be victorious in the defeat of Saddam. And every man should return to his home and ensure that his sons and daughters were not influenced by the work of the devil being spread from satellite television screens. Local television was acceptable, he said, knowing that it was strictly limited to controlled progaganda channels. What I objected to was the fact that these Imams were brainwashing our parents into controlling their children, holding them back to a mediaeval life, while the outside world soared on. Whenever my father returned from the mosque I would notice how quiet and confused he seemed. He had, after all, spent more than 20 years in the West, drinking, smoking, mixing with Western friends who went to the races, cursed and watched all manner of shows on TV. Some of those teachings had clearly hit home with my father, evidenced by the lack of satellite TV and no telephone.

At the office the following day I saw two men in the corridor with Zana. They were Westerners, dressed in cargo pants and T-shirts, but they also understood Kurdish because I just happened to catch Zana telling them: 'Be careful what you say when she's around because she speaks English.' They nodded and made their way out, but when I heard them speaking to one another as they left the building it was German they were using. It was a curious interlude and I never found out who they were but I thought it interesting that they should have been present at a time when Zana was asking me to work as a spy. Were they spies as well?

My problem was that I had come so far with Zana that I now could not back out of anything that he asked me to do. I knew too much: that this company of his was more than just a construction company. I thought of it more as an intelligence-gathering centre, although I never really knew whether the employees, who were all related, were in on it. At least I felt that the men must have been.

Each time my aunt was in the building, Zana left me to continue my office duties, retyping old typewritten documents into the computer so that the records could be stored as data.

A few days after my bizarre driving lessons and while my aunt was away, Zana drove me to the Jyan Hotel. It was where all the foreigners stayed or called in for a drink or a meal and where they held casual business meetings. It also had a reputation as a pick-up joint for expensive prostitutes from Turkey. Zana knew everything about the place. As we sat on the plush lobby sofas I became concerned about being there, worried that someone would tell my father. He told me not to worry—people who came to the Jyan would not know my father. He pointed out a diplomat, a company director, an oil executive from the Arab side of the Kurdish line and prostitute after prostitute.

I wondered if he used them but as if to read my thoughts he

laughed and said: 'You soon learn to pick them.'

I ordered an Arab version of Coca-Cola and then we were joined by a Swede, working for an NGO (non-governmental organisation) building a hospital in the area, who had brought along a male interpreter. I don't know why either I or the other interpreter was needed because both the Swede and Zana spoke English. Zana introduced me to the Swede as the receptionist and administration officer from his company and, taking a hint, I pulled out a notebook from my bag—I usually carried one around for sketching rather than note taking—but went through the motions of recording the conversation.

At one stage during their chatter, Zana turned to me to ask a question about a house we had set land aside for. Was it two storeys or three, he wanted to know. I had no idea what he was talking about. I was sure the house didn't exist but not wanting to embarrass either him or me, I said: 'That's the two-storey one. We've yet to complete the plans for the bigger property.'

Later, as we drove back to the office, I asked Zana what that had all been about.

'It was your initiative test,' he said. 'I wanted to see how quickly you latched onto the situation—suddenly being introduced as an adminstration officer—and realising the need to immediately start taking notes. Your answer about the house was excellent, seeing that neither exist.'

'And did I pass my test?' I asked, trying to hide the sarcasm in my voice, for I felt I had been used.

'Yes,' he said with a grin. 'You passed.'

'I assume you don't want these notes, then.'

'You can throw them away as soon as we get back.'

He drove on for a while before speaking again. 'Not only was it important for you to reveal to me that you can handle a situation that is suddenly thrust upon you, I wanted you to see that hotel. I wanted you to see the false smiles of everybody, because believe me they are false. I wanted you to see how they are all feeding off one another. It's nothing but a nest of vipers and many of those people you saw today are going to get bitten by poison.'

Welcome to more of the joys of Kurdistan, I thought.

There was one final lesson for me, before I was to embark on my spying mission. In between times, I had spoken to David, each time feeling that warm glow covering me as I heard his voice. I told him I was trying to find a way to come out to his house to see him again because I was missing him so much. That was true. I really was missing him. The time gap since I'd last seen him had curiously drawn me closer to him.

'We have to go out into the desert again,' said Zana as he led me to his car for my final training session. I was expecting a freshening-up course in my driving. But what came was a big jump forward and left me in no doubt about the dangers Zana knew might lie ahead.

When we climbed from his car in the middle of nowhere he led me away from the car—then brought a handgun from his bag. A moment of panic rushed over me. Alone in the desert with a man, the mountains to the north and east, too far away from the car for me to run and drive off, now that I knew how to drive.

'Have you ever fired one of these?' he asked, holding out what he said was a Russian-made pistol.

'I've never even touched one,' I said. 'We didn't go around shooting things in Sydney.'

He ignored the comment. 'By the time we leave here today you will know all about this weapon and you'll also be able to hit a target.'

Zana placed a large green apple, an import from Syria, on top of a rock.

'I'm going to teach you how to shoot. First, give me a demonstraton.'

He gave the gun to me, made me stand about 10 metres from the target and told me to gently squeeze the trigger. I tried to remember what I'd seen on TV, how the police used to hold their guns with two hands. In fact, it was so heavy that I had to use both hands in any case. So I did the same and pulled the trigger. The crack of the weapon rang out across the desert. The apple was untouched.

He nodded as though he expected that was how I would stand and how I would miss. Then he gave me his instructions, showing me how to use one hand underneath the other—not side by side—as a support and how to wrap my thumb around the top rear of the gun and not have it sticking out. In effect, I had to use the left hand as a support while the right hand did the aiming and pulled the trigger. As for my body, it was all about balance. My legs should not be straight and side by side. Rather, they had to be slightly bent, with one leg slightly forward.

By the end of the morning I had successfully destroyed our lunch. The bag of apples he had brought, the gun-smashed pieces lying on the hot desert sand were testimony to my newly-acquired skill.

'What are you getting me into, Zana?' I asked—a question I seemed to be putting to him frequently. His answer was the same. Being able to drive and shoot were priceless skills and I should be grateful to have acquired them. I asked what the point of learning to drive and shoot was if I didn't have a car or a gun.

'I can't get you a car because that would be obvious and stupid, but I can get you a gun.'

'I don't want one,' I said.

'When—if—you do, let me know.'

A few days later I spoke to David at his office, calling from the company phone. This time it was not a secret call. Zana was standing right behind me. I told David that I had a chance of being dropped off at his house by the office driver who was going to the area and that I had explained to the driver I needed to pick up documents. David was ecstatic that I was coming around. But there was no involvement by the office driver. It was Zana who drove me to the big UN house with the fluttering flags.

On the way he asked me to open the glove box. I brought out a white cloth wrapped around something heavy. I knew exactly what it was. A gun.

'Zana, what do you expect me to do with this?' I asked with sudden alarm.

'Are you expecting me to use it on—'

'Don't be silly. I don't want you to shoot your boyfriend. It's for you to hang on to.'

'I don't want it. I can't keep it for a start. Do you think I'm going to walk into my father's house with a gun. If he found it what would he think? Worse, what would he do?'

'I'll keep it at the office for you, then,' said Zana. 'If the time ever comes—'

'The time will never come, Zana,' I said.

At the UN house, I jumped from the car and, as with the first time I had been there, I entered through the kitchen, nodding a hello to the Assyrian housekeeper again. This was to be a two-pronged visit, while Zana remained parked down a laneway. I had to draw David closer to me—and that would not be so difficult because I truly wanted him to be closer—but I also had to look around, check out the lie of the land so to speak, and look at any documents that might be lying about. I felt like a rat. I was on a mission of love and deceit.

'Latifa!' David cried when I knocked on his lounge room door and entered. He jumped from his sofa and came towards me, arms outstretched. We hugged and kissed and then he invited me to sit down—in front of a huge cheese cake that he said he'd asked a colleague to bring from Baghdad the day before.

'It's fate,' he said. 'I didn't even know you would be able to come. This is a special celebration indeed.'

So we ate cheesecake and then he showed me around his house, but there wasn't much to see. The three bedrooms were basically empty, one being used to store a gas canister and an electricity generator and the other had his bed. But it was not until we returned to the lounge that I felt his arms wrap around me from behind and then he turned me and kissed me. I've read it in novels—how a girl feels like she is melting in the arms of a man—and that is exactly how I felt then. But I was scared, too. I didn't want this to go too far. Not because I was afraid of losing my virginity—it was a bit late for that!

'Can we move just a little more slowly, David,' I said as we caressed. 'I don't want to get pregnant.'

'Don't worry, that won't happen. I am well prepared. You will be safe.'

That convinced me and we made love. It was the passion I had desperately longed for. It was wonderful to be touched and there was a thrill about it because it was forbidden. I was totally smitten by this man and all thoughts of betraying him by trying to look through his documents vanished. In any case, how was I to carry out my mission for Zana with David present? I had noticed his brief case, propped up on the floor beside a chair when I had entered the room, but there was no opportunity to look into it—even if the desire to do so had been there.

So David had become my second lover after Ojo. I do not count Mikael as a lover—he was a rapist. As much as I wanted to stay, I told David shortly afterwards that I had to leave. Two hours had passed and he did not know that Zana was waiting in his car down the lane. I couldn't tell him that, of course, nor could I tell him that I had a company driver on stand by because that would have been equally suspicious. As if he realised my concern about how I would get back to the office, he arranged for one of his drivers to drop me there. We kissed goodbye for the time being, with me telling him I would try to see him again as soon as possible, and then his driver took me to the office. I then had to ask the company driver to take me back to the laneway where Zana was still waiting. It was crazy, but it was the only way. Zana made some excuse to the company driver about why he was sitting in his car in the laneway.

'So how did it go?' asked Zana as we headed back. 'Did you manage to find out anything?'

'It was impossible. He was with me the whole time.'

'But did you see any documents lying around? Is he the kind of person that leaves papers on a table, that kind of thing?'

'I didn't see anything like that. There wasn't really any opportunity.'

'Well you must try, do your best, it's very important.'

I felt terrible. Depressed that I had been so betrayed by my mother, I was now doing the same thing with a man that, yes, I had to admit it, I had fallen in love with.

Zana continued to ask me about David's house, what it was like inside, how many rooms it had and so on. 'That's a typical UN house,' he said. 'Big and bleak with a housekeeper. Does he have a fax machine in there?'

'No, just a telephone. I didn't see any other technical things if that's what you mean.'

'Well, you don't seem to have got much from this visit.'

'Zana, I can't just walk in there and start picking up documents or writing things down. As far as he was concerned, it was a social visit by me. I need more time for this.'

His face hardened. 'Just remember this,' he said. 'Your time is not important. You are working in our time. It is our time that is important, not yours.'

I didn't ask who he meant by 'our', although I assumed it was the Kurdish authorities.

With Zana's knowledge, I was now able to keep in daily contact with David and it was soon arranged for me to go back to his house. This time Zana sent me there with the company driver and it was agreed he would return for me after a couple of hours. David had decided to send his Assyrian housekeeper home early after she had completed her morning chores, telling her to return later in the afternoon.

This time David and I did not hesitate with our love making. Again, it was on the sofa, but it was at my initiative. Afterwards, unlike my first visit when there was more of an urgency about our intimacy and my having to leave, he asked if I wanted to take a shower with him. I told him I would shower when I got home, so he slipped away to wash.

With trembling hands, I went to his briefcase when I heard the shower running. I made a quick note of the fax numbers across the top of the pages I found and also wrote down names of the senders. There was no time to read through the documents and find out what the contents were—some were written in English, others in Arabic—although the general tone appeared to be of a technical nature. While I could not understand spoken Arabic, I could read the written symbols. There was a map of a village in Syria, some architectural designs, and a few pages in handwriting that I assumed was David's. I had not been asked by Zana to read through the documents in any case. He simply wanted phone and fax numbers and names.

I heard the shower stop running, made sure there was nothing amiss with his papers or the positioning of the briefcase, and returned to the sofa. Soon afterwards I was on my way back to the office with the information. I wondered if this was how those Russian spy girls controlled their emotions. Those honey traps they set. I wondered if they ever fell in love with their diplomatic and commercial targets or whether they remained cold hearted and treated their various missions as just another job. For me, what I was doing was a passage out of Kurdistan. I was pleasing Zana and I was pleasing David. Both had promised to help me, Zana because I was giving him something back; David because he had fallen for me, of that I had no doubt. The only disturbing element was that I had also fallen for David and I felt wretched each time I remembered my spying mission.

On my fourth visit to David, with the same routine occurring—he going to the shower, me rifling through his papers—he said he wanted to ask me something as I prepared to leave. My heart missed several beats as he went to his briefcase and pulled out a handful of documents.

He held them up in front of me. Dear God.

ELEVEN

'These documents,' he said. 'Not only do I have to cope with all these, as though that's not enough, but I've also lost my interpreter who's been shifted to do another job. So I'd like to ask you Latifa—will you work for me as my interpreter?'

I don't know whether my face revealed my relief but I could not stifle a gasp.

He grinned. 'You seem overwhelmed. I hope you aren't going to turn me down!'

I hugged him, unable to prevent the tears welling up. Working as David's interpreter would tear my heart open even more. I would be drawn even closer to him, there was no doubt about that, but the job would also give me access to all his paperwork and allow me to be present at all his meetings. I would, like the suspicions I had about my mother, be the perfect spy—an interpreter with access to all the information that an outside party wanted.

When I saw my father that evening I told him about the job offer. His response shocked me.

'Work for the UN? Oh no. I will never allow any daughter of mine to work for them. All the girls who work for the UN are nothing but whores. They have a shocking reputation. They mingle with foreigners and they sleep with them. They defy the love of their parents. They leave for work in the *hijab* but as soon as they arrive at the office they put on their mini skirts and their lipstick and they make themselves available to anyone and everyone.'

'But Dad, don't assume that I'm like that. And the pay would be very good. I'm told I could earn up to $US500 a month.'

That was, in fact, an excellent wage in a country where $US1 would buy enough fruit and vegetables to feed an entire family.

'In any case,' Khalid continued. 'Money is not our problem. My project is working out well.'

He had told me previously about the contract his welding company had received. The Mayor of Dohuk had asked my father to build a tourist attraction on a large area of land that would comprise restaurants, a children's playground, a convenience store and even a small botanical garden. Many of the employees working on the project were his own relatives. 'Always look after your own first,' he constantly told me. The money he would be making in the summer, he said, would more than easily cover the slack winter months.

I knew that any attempt at getting my father to change his attitude about the UN job would be futile. Not only did he dissuade me from ever talking back at him, he was a stubborn man and he was a far less relaxed father than the one I had known in Sydney. His turning to the Muslim faith had changed him and I suspected, too, that he was still upset about the break up of his marriage. I heard chatter among my aunts one day about my mother 'seeing another man' in Germany, but I didn't hear any more details.

When I called David about my father's refusal, he was disappointed. We agreed we would try to meet as often as possible, but the irony was that the only way I could get any transport to see him was when Zana arranged it for me so that I could actually spy on David. I had no idea of the value of the information I was passing on to Zana, whenever I could get hold of anything new, that was. All that I was able to pick up from David's briefcase and from any papers that might have been lying around were names and phone numbers, but often they were the same ones over and over again.

Warning signs were beginning to sound, though. My approach to my father about working as an interpreter had prompted a question the following day.

'Aren't you happy working with your aunt and Zana at the company? You should be grateful that you have a job there, because you are surrounded by relatives, unlike if you were working for the UN.'

It sounded innocent enough, but I knew my father well enough to know that problems could lie ahead.

How grateful I was for the company of the sisters across the road. On my days off on Fridays and when the men were at the mosque, I would snatch the opportunity to meet them in their house and chat, with me doing most of the talking, telling them about my life in Australia and describing some of the well-known sights in Sydney. I described the famous bridge and Opera House and they sat around in a circle and listened in awe. They could see how much I was missing it all and assured me that they were praying for me each day, asking God to open the door so I could return to Australia.

As the weeks rolled by, reports continued to spread around Kurdistan about the inevitability of war. The UN weapons inspectors were having trouble getting permission to travel around Iraq and George W Bush was threatening an attack if Saddam Hussein did not co-operate. I spoke to David frequently and also saw him from time to time whenever Zana felt it was worth another look at his documents in case I could find any new names.

There were times when David had to travel to Baghdad or Jordan, always returning with gifts for me, including my favourite perfumes, Chanel No. 5 and 24 Fauburg, but I had to be careful to wear them only when I was with him. I had to wash the perfume from my neck when I left because my aunties and my grandmother would be certain to smell it and ask where it had come from. He even brought me back a sexy DD bra, after first checking my size. He was a giver, a man of great charm and I hated using him to please Zana because I loved him.

However, Zana was beginning to show impatience. He told me that I just wasn't bringing him enough useful information. I asked how that was possible if all I could find were the documents in David's briefcase.

'There's another way to find out what they're up to,' he said and I braced myself for his next suggestion.

'We want to find out who he's talking to on the phone and what the discussions are all about.'

'Well,' I said, 'he's more likely to be doing that in his office. There's no way I'm going to be able to get an invite there because he doesn't want his staff to know that he's been seeing me. And even if I got there, do you honestly believe he's going to chat away on the phone, discussing all kinds of UN things with me sitting around? Even if I was working with him as an interpreter, he wouldn't want me listening in to his phone conversation which might be of a more secretive nature.'

Zana studied me as I spoke. 'What you have just said reveals to me, once again Latifa, that you are the right woman for this work. You have assessed what "we" have already agreed on. We've talked it over and we believe that what we've decided is something that you can do without running into any kind of trouble.'

I suddenly thought about the driving lessons and the shooting practice. Was he now dragging me towards dangerous waters?

'There are two steps to go through. The first will be a test run. The second will be the real thing.'

Zana's 'first step' was a phone call he made to David. His company, he told David when he knew he was at his office, had completed all the plans for the tender for the pipeline project and would it be convenient to send Latifa around to drop them off? Of course, David agreed. So around to the UN compound I went and met David in his office. He was delighted to see me but we did not embrace, with other staff members moving about. As we chatted generally, standing in the middle of his office, I made a mental note of the layout, just as Zana had requested. He was coming and going with staff asking him to check this and that, so I had an opportunity to look around his office. Then, at last, when I laid the plans out on the desk I suddenly exclaimed that one of the sheets was missing. This again was according to Zana's plan—but poor David thought it was something I had engineered so I could see him again when I brought the missing page back.

Returning to the company's office, I told Zana that I thought I had noticed a good place to hide a voice recorder. When he discussed the new spying venture he had planned for me he said he wanted me to plant a recorder somewhere in David's office. He showed me the gadget. It was a Sanyo digital recorder with a voice activation switch and a running time of many hours. Zana explained that when arrangements had been made for me to return to David's office, it would already be switched on and while it would pick up the sounds of me travelling there and any conversations I would have with David, it would also pick up anything he said in his office in my absence. All I had to do was conceal it somewhere!

The following day I was driven back to the UN compound with the 'missing' page of the pipeline project. It genuinely gave David and me the chance to chat. I had the recorder in my bag so I was careful to not make my conversations with him too romantic. Although Zana knew, or had certainly guessed, that David and I were in a relationship, I didn't want any recorded conversation between us to end up in the wrong hands—like my father's.

I thought I might know where I could plant the device, but I needed David to be out of the office. I had thought of a plan which might work. I asked if he had a small notepad because my diary was full and I wanted to keep a record of my daily activities. If he had something with UN on it, a constant reminder of him, so much the better. He checked in his desk drawer, fumbled around and said he had to go to the storeroom to get what he thought would be the very thing. As soon as he left the room I hurried across to the desk because it was the very place that I had decided, on my previous visit when I had managed to idly wander around as I talked to him, I would hide the recorder. I had noticed a gap between the drawer and the side of the desk—a space like a small open-ended box. Now I put my hand into it to see how deep it was and was surprised to find that the space ran around behind the back of the drawer. Perfect. Even if David looked into the gap beside the drawer he would not see the recorder. He would have to pull the drawer right out to find it and I doubted whether he would be doing anything like that. So into that hiding place I put the recorder. Although now encased in wood, I hoped it would still be able to pick up his voice when he spoke on the phone, which was on his desk.

By the time he returned—thankfully he had been called into another room on his way back from the storeroom—I was comfortably seated away from the desk. He handed me a nice leather-bound notebook which the UN used as a promotional gift. Inside he had written my name, along with the words: For My Love, followed by his name.

'David,' I asked softly as I was leaving, 'is there any more news about me? Have you been able to make any inquiries about how I can get a passport?'

'It's taking a little while, but don't worry. Things will be all right, Latifa. Just be patient. Don't dwell on it or the time will drag by. Wait until I have good news for you.' He gave my hand a quick squeeze.

As the company driver took me back I realised the great risk I had taken. Suppose the UN's tea boy had walked in as I was fumbling around with David's desk? It had been a big risk, but I'd gotten away with it.

Zana was pleased with my success, but said it was now important that I get the recorder back the following day. Of course, I had to recover it! I hadn't even thought about that. How was I to make yet another excuse to go back to David's office? As it transpired, it was David who called saying he'd like to see me again because he'd forgotten to give me some calligraphy pens that went with the notebook he'd given me.

'I'll find an excuse to come over and pick them up,' I said. 'I'll tell Zana that I've left my personal diary behind over there and that I need to get it back. I'm sure he'll let me come over.'

I was getting myself tangled in lies. I had to pretend to David that I was pretending something else to Zana—while Zana was of course delighted that I'd received the invitation to return to the UN office.

'Be careful, Latifa,' I told myself. 'Don't get into a mess.'

I felt like I was riding on a fast train to an unknown destination, travelling with passengers who all knew one another but weren't acknowledging it. Would the train crash on the way, destroying us all, or would we reach the destination and be able to run free?

At the compound, David was sitting behind his desk, the gift box of pens in front of him. He rose to formally shake my hand—the most daring form of romance we could show—then returned to his chair. He propped his arms on the desk. His elbows were half a metre from the hidden recorder. I tried to remain calm as I thought: 'How am I going to get him out of the office? I've got to get it back.'

Then another thought struck me. Didn't recorders make squealing sounds when the batteries, or the tape, or the small disc or whatever operating system it was, ran out? David asked how things were and, aware that the recorder would be picking up our voices, I told him that I was happy working at the company with my aunt helping me and other relatives coming and going. He seemed surprised at my words because I had told him at the beginning of our friendship how unhappy I was and what a deadly situation I was in. Quickly and playfully and with a big smile on my face I skipped around the desk, put my lips to his ear and whispered: 'Only kidding!' He thought it was funny and grinned. I was about to give him a kiss when one of his office-bound interpreters popped his head around the door to say that an Arab-speaking person wanted to have a word with David and the interpreter would have to act as a go between.

David excused himself, but told me he'd be back in a moment to say goodbye. It was my chance!

I slipped around behind the desk and felt in through the gap. I couldn't find the device! Had it been on the right side or the left that I'd pushed it through? I got on my knees and slid my hand through the gap on the other edge of the desk and felt around behind the drawer. No it wasn't there. Back to the other side and this time I reached in further. There it was. But in my fumbling I'd managed to push it slightly further away. Sweat bubbled up on my brow. I couldn't reach it! I'd have to pull the drawer right out! But no, I could hear David talking in the hallway outside. He was coming back! I wanted to scream. My finger was flicking against the edge of the recorder, as I tried to draw it back into a position where I could grab it. When all seemed lost I managed to pull it out. My bag was on the other side of the room. If I'd carried it to the desk David might have wondered why. I pulled the top of my blouse open and quickly stuffed the slim device into the top of my bra before jumping to my feet and spinning around to pretend I was looking out of a nearby window.

I'm sure my face must have been white with fear or bright red with soaring blood pressure. I kept my back to David as he entered the room, pretending that I was looking at the distant mountains. He came and stood behind me.

'At least the view's nice,' he said. 'But I don't recommend the honeymoon suite.'

Well, that comment went on the tape, but then, whoever heard it aside from Zana might think it was the UN man's way of complaining about his accommodation.

Back at the office, Zana grabbed the recorder from me without a word of thanks and said he was leaving for the day. I assumed he was taking it to his friends in the government. I wondered what they would hear on it, whether David's conversations would reveal great secrets, but I was never to find out.

There was a genuine reason for me to return to David's office several days later. I had to deliver a final schedule for the company's tender relating to the pipeline project. David had already told me that a number of our competitors had been dismissed because they were either not up to the task or they were too expensive. This time I called at the house, a request that he had made and which Zana, expecting some good news about the project, agreed to.

But instead of a smiling David, he seemed upset and a little cold towards me. He'd found out about the recorder! Was there a hidden security camera in the office? Had I dropped something beside the desk? Had he found the device, replaced it and then talked nonsense to a make-believe acquaintance? Almost daily something happened to scare me. For at home I was still having to turn down requests from mothers who came knocking at the door asking permission for me to marry their sons. I was in danger of becoming a mental wreck and until now it had only been David's love that had kept me on an even keel. Now, as I looked at his face, I feared my world was about to totally collapse.

I walked to him and gently took his hands.

'What's wrong?'

'I have a problem—and it does involve you.'

No, no.

'I need you to put my mind at rest.'

It would not have been difficult to see the alarm on my face.

'Don't worry, it's not you directly, Latifa. It's about work and it's really distracting me. I have narrowed down the pipeline project to two companies, one of which is yours, or rather the one you're working for. The problem is, your competitors' proposal is the better by far. I have to make my recommendations by tomorrow. If I recommend your competitor, it means I won't have any excuses to see you. I don't want that to happen, but on the other hand, I don't want to give the project to your company, which hasn't come up to the required standard.'

I wasn't surprised by that. I had already concluded that Zana's company was a government front. But I also now realised that part of my spying mission was to find out what David was thinking in terms of the pipeline project. The mission would not have related to that alone, however. Many of the documents I had seen concerned other projects within Iraq itself and Zana and his compatriates had wanted to know about everything for their own political reasons.

'David, you cannot risk your own position for my sake. You have to be professional and you must recommend the other company. It would be entirely wrong to suggest Zana's company solely because you want to see me. Don't worry, we will work it out. We will find a way to keep seeing each other.'

But even as I spoke those words, I wondered how. We made love again and I cried because I worried that this might be the last time.

When, three days later, Zana learned that the company had failed to win the pipeline project, he moped about the office and kept away from me. It was as though he was blaming me for the failure because it was I, after all, who was in regular touch—for all the wrong reasons—with the UN man who made the decision.

The loss of the project caused turmoil within the office. My aunt suddenly announced to me that we were going home early—and that we would not be returning. Ever.

On the way home, I asked her what was going on.

'It's none of your business, but I'll be working for the government on a rebuilding project. That means that your job with Zana is over. If I'm not going to be there, you're not going to be there.'

'But that's not fair. You decide to leave and you kill my job. That's not right at all.'

'Your father will not allow you to continue working there without me. It was because of me being employed there that you got the job in the first place. Now it's over.'

I was so distressed that as I made to get out of the car at my father's house and she asked if I was going to kiss her goodbye, I said: 'You should give yourself a kiss for the success you've had this afternoon.'

I was embittered because not only had a rift come between David and me with the loss of the project, the loss of my job—my only link with him because he knew where to ring me—had now become a gaping chasm. I was now standing on one side and he, and my grasp at freedom, was on the other. And what of Zana's promise to me? A promise, on the Koran, that he would be able to get me out of Kurdistan without any documents. How was I now to contact him unless he came to me with news? But I knew in my heart that wasn't going to happen. Well, he had sworn on the Koran to help. God would know whether to punish him or not.

When my father returned home from work I told him what had happened. 'That's very good,' he said, adding, 'that your aunt has got a good job. She'll be very happy working for the government.'

He made no comment on the loss of my job, except to say that it would be good to have me home again during the day because I could help my grandmother with the house. There was no suggestion at all that I could continue at the company. It went without saying that my employment there was over.

The following day, to my amazement, Zana and one of the company owners—who I was certain was more than just an 'owner' or director—came to the door when my father was at home. They asked for me to be present when they sat down to address him.

'Brother,' Zana said to my father, 'I hold great respect for you and I come to speak about your daughter. Latifa is a very good asset for our company. She is very efficient with the computer, with the paperwork and in answering the telephone. Her language skills are unequalled compared to anyone else we have ever employed there. We would like her to continue and we will ensure that at all times she is safe in our care.'

He had hardly finished when my father began shaking his head. 'I appreciate your comments, but it cannot be. Without her aunty, there, she cannot be there.'

Zana started again while I was sent away to bring tea, but my father kept his head down—a sign that no matter what they said to him, the answer would remain no. They could implore him all morning but that hung head would be a constant negative. It was obvious to me why they wanted me to continue working there. I had proved to be their perfect spy.

Zana tried a different tactic. 'Latifa has proved herself to be so efficient that I believe she has been offered a job as an interpreter at the UN. Perhaps, brother, that would be a good opportunity for her. Her efficiency, with respect to you, should not be wasted, and the money is good.'

'She's not being wasted,' my father said, raising his head at last. 'You know and I know, brother, the reputation those women have. The money is not important. You can never buy back a lost reputation, no matter how pure she remains.'

'What if she had a relative in the UN? Would that make a difference for you?'

'No female relative of mine will be lowered to work for them. Even if there was a cousin there, I would still not allow it.'

Zana nodded, conceding he was getting nowhere. I was astonished that this conversation was taking place in front of me, as though I wasn't even there.

When at last I escorted the two visitors to the door, I managed to whisper to Zana: 'Please don't forget your promise to me.'

He looked puzzled. 'What promise?'

My heart sank.

TWELVE

In my room I wanted to scream and scream, but I didn't want anyone to hear what I knew they would consider a sign of weakness and victory—theirs. So I pulled a rag across my mouth and buried my head in the pillow and yelled and cried out. It wasn't the first time, a reaction to my feelings of utter rejection and despair.

After a while I decided to call Zana, who would by now be back at the office. My father had gone out so I seized the chance to hurry across to my neighbours' home. I told my grandmother, as usual, I was just going to 'see the girls across the road for a minute or two'. Even so, she went out into the garden to check that the boys weren't on the neighbouring roof before she gave a nod of assent.

When I knocked on the girls' door they were surprised to see me, asking if I was supposed to be at work. I explained what had happened and that even the offer of a UN interpreter's job had been turned down by my father.

'Oh, you wouldn't want to work for them,' said the oldest sister. 'The women who work for the UN have a very bad reputation.'

So even they had heard. I suggested it might just have been a bad rumour that had spread without any foundation and that they should give the women the benefit of the doubt. Then I asked to use the phone.

When I was put through to Zana I asked why he had not worked harder on my father to get my job back. 'You should know, Latifa, that when your father says no, he means no.'

'What about your promise to me? You seem to have forgotten all about it. Yet you swore on the Koran you would help me.'

There was silence for a few moments, then he asked me to call him back in five minutes. The sisters could see the frustation on my face, although they had not understood my conversation, which had been in English. When I called Zana back, he assured me the promise still held good and that I would still be able to work for him in the meantime. That meant, of course, I might be able to remain in touch with David, even though the pipeline contract had failed to materialise.

'But what about my father?' I said. 'You saw how negative he was so what makes you think he'll change his mind when you go back to him?'

'It's a new proposal altogether. There's an opening for you in Erbil. There are other women working there. Your father will approve if he knows you're in the company of women.'

Erbil, he explained, was the town east of the large city of Mosul where the Kurdistan parliament was located and where there was a more open attitude to the West. 'It will take you away from the restraints of your family,' he said.

'How is that going to be possible?' I asked. 'My father will not accept me living in a different town.'

'The only way, then, is for you to just leave. . . just slip away with us.'

'Who's "us"?'

'The company, of course. You will be in our care. There will be plenty of jobs you can do, similar to what you've been doing here.'

'Oh, you mean—'

He cut me short before I could use the word 'spy'. But he went on to say that Erbil was also the town where Arab politicians talked to the Kurds.

'What do you want me to do this time, Zana, sleep with Udai and Qusai, Saddam's sons?' I asked bitterly.

He laughed at his own reply: 'Oh no, of course not, but if you do sleep with Arabs, don't kiss them on the ears because that's where they put poison. But listen, sister, seriously, do your best to persuade your father. You will get your own car and apartment. I don't mean that you will have to drive your car because that would be expecting too much, but you'll have your own driver. If you can do this last thing for us, you'll be home safe in Australia very soon.'

Something told me to turn this down, even if I could talk my father into starting work for Zana again. I thought the chances of him agreeing were against me and even asking might infuriate him when he would have expected me to know how he would react.

It happened that my aunt Hadar from Baghdad, who I got on well with despite that lecherous husband of hers, was visiting Dohuk and I asked her if we could go to tea somewhere together while she was there. We found a small place where we could talk, on the pretext to my father and grandmother that we were going to do some shopping.

I told her about Zana's proposal and asked her advice. A strict Muslim who received all her guidance from the Koran, she said that before I approached my father I should turn to the Holy Book.

It would give me the answers I sought. There were two answers, of course. Should I approach my father and if there was a positive response, should I accept Zana's offer? The Koran would tell me, she assured me, telling me to open it at random and if my eyes fell upon a *surat* (verse) that was in any way negative—whether it talked about punishment, things that were frightening, anything that I understood to mean a 'downer'—to see that as a message not to even ask my father. But if the *surat* was cheerful, talking perhaps about God having a river of honey in paradise or referring to angels, then I should speak to my father about the job offer.

It seemed crazy to me, that my future should depend on the fall of a page, but that evening I brought down a Koran from its resting place on top of my closet—the book must always be kept in a high place if possible—and sat with it on my knee. When I had first arrived in Kurdistan my father had given the book to me, each page divided into three colums. The first was the Arabic script, the middle column was the pronunciation and the third was the translation. I closed my eyes and opened it, placing my finger on a page. The words told how disbelievers would be burned in hell fire.

That was no good, but anxious to get that job I thought I would try again, in case I had accidentally let a page slip through my fingers and had missed more positive verses. The second time was another reference to sinners burning in hell, with a particular reference to women who showed their hair or cleavage. There was a reference there, too, to Lot's wife who turned into a pillar of salt as she fled from Sodom and Gomorrah. That was enough. I wouldn't speak to my father.

I called Zana from the neighbours' phone and told him that on divine guidance—which surprised him—I could not take the job. He urged me to think again and even offered to get a mobile phone to me so that I could call him if I changed my mind. He was obviously eager for me to go to Erbil but I was also aware that I could be letting myself into something particularly dangerous this time. Otherwise, why all that shooting practice and fast driving lessons?

'Don't throw away your chance,' he said and I realised he was referring to my hopes of escaping. But a wave of doubt had come over me. I had done his dirty work for him once and now he was dangling the 'escape carrot' again in return for another 'mission'.

'Zana, I'm sorry, but I don't feel I can trust your promises any more. I'll think about it, but I doubt whether I'm going to talk to my father about this.'

I remained in my room for much of the following two days, coming out just to eat. George W Bush was gearing up for war and it was a topic on everyone's lips but all I could think about was my own broken heart over the possibility of not seeing David again and also the job in Erbil that I had failed to follow up on with my father. I was so confused. And I was still trapped, with mothers still calling by with offers of marriage from sons I could not even recall ever meeting. This place, this whole region, was a madhouse.

David would have been wondering what had happened to me as I hadn't been in touch since losing my job. I had considered calling him from the neighbours' but I knew that hearing his voice would have only added to my frustration at not being able to be with him. Finally I talked myself into it.

'Latifa, what's happened. I called your office and they said you didn't work there any more.'

When I explained the situation, he urged me to be patient; there would be a way of us seeing one another. I asked if there was any more news for me about leaving but he said I had to continue to be patient. Patient, patient. I'd had enough of being patient. Every day brought new misery and fear. 'Please, please, David, try to do something. Have you not been able to contact anyone? Surely you

156

could just pick up your phone and call the Australian Embassy in Baghdad. I can't do it from this phone—its got a bar on making long distance calls.'

He said he was still working on it, but he'd been flat out and he needed to talk to me in detail about my background and have my passport number ready when he contacted the embassy. I hadn't yet passed those details to him. I arranged to call him the following day—and I had thought up a scheme that might urge him to work more quickly on my case, while bringing me closer to him.

It had been several weeks since we had first made love without using any protection.

'David. . . I think I'm pregnant.'

The silence I expected followed.

Then: 'Are you sure, Latifa? It seems so. . . soon.'

'It may seem soon but I'm late.'

'I see.'

What he said next really shocked me.

'Are you sure it's mine?'

I exploded. 'What do you mean by that? What kind of woman do you think I am? I love you, David, I haven't been with anybody in Iraq, if that's what you're suggesting. Just because I was raped back in Germany doesn't mean that I'm anybody's. You've really hurt me.'

He was apologetic. 'I'm sorry. It's come as such a shock. We obviously need to talk about this. I've got a very important assignment that's going to tie me up for the next three days. Call me in exactly four days and we'll take this further.'

Once again I felt like a heel. But was my scheme beginning to reveal David's true feelings? He was obviously very fond of me but he had never told me he loved me. Then again, I had never said those words to him, either, but he must surely have guessed that I was just

157

crazy about him, despite my betrayal in spying on him. I remained stunned at his suggestion that I had been sleeping around. Had he forgotten how difficult it was to even see him on occasions?

I called his office as arranged on the fourth day, only to receive another shock. David was in Jordan. He'd left two days before—and he wouldn't be back for a month. I refused to believe that he had skipped the country to wait out confirmation whether or not I was pregnant. But the thought lingered at the back of my mind.

I found out he had returned to Dohuk after four weeks when I saw him on the 6pm local news. He was shown talking to the local mayor about all the building projects the UN would be sponsoring around the city. When I called him the first thing he asked was:

'Are you pregnant?'

I told him I was not. But ironically, I had been late that month, until things returned to normal. He apologised for rushing off to Jordan so suddenly but an urgent matter had come up and he had no way of contacting me or leaving a message specially for me. I wondered about his excuse, but my love for him overwhelmed my doubts. We agreed that I would work out a way of seeing him. It might be days, it might be weeks, I told him, but he could expect me at any time.

Winter was setting in. Snow covered the mountain tops and a cruel wind swept through the narrow streets of Dohuk bringing rain and sleet. Now many of the men were wearing scarfs, too, wrapping the woollen pieces of cloth around their heads and faces—a taste of what women had to put up with every day of the year! George W Bush was beating his war drum and Saddam Hussein was remaining defiant.

An older cousin, Areeman, would come to stay with us for a few days, replacing my grandmother with the cooking chores when my grandmother was away visiting relatives for a few days in Mosul and picking up her pension of 450 dinars a month. Along with Areeman came two of her sisters, aged 16 and 14, as well as her younger brother, who was about my age. Areeman was the daughter of one of my father's sisters and she had had a hard time of it at school with a tummy that bulged abnormally, giving rise to constant talk that she was pregnant and a wicked girl to be avoided. The poor thing could not help her condition and had learned to live with the jibes. I enjoyed her company and when my father was out we would dress up in my bedroom in clothes we were not allowed to wear in public. One day we made ourselves up to look like seductive Arab women, seductive eyes staring into the camera I had been amazingly allowed to keep. With another cousin—making a respectable group of three—we went into town and had the film processed and watched as the pictures rolled off the drying drum to ensure that none went astray and ended up doing the rounds of the tea shops. We laughed hysterically at the pictures. For me the dressing up had been a tonic for it gave me just a taste of the life I had left so long ago, it seemed, in the West. I was now 22—another year to add to my age and another step closer to the time when my father would inevitably say: 'You've waited long enough for a husband and now I'm going to find one for you.'

One morning, while Areeman was still staying in the house with her sisters and brother, and in my father's absence, I decided I could stand the absence from David no longer. I told her I had to get out of the house for an hour or so—alone.

'Are you crazy?' she exclaimed.

When I told her it was for strong personal reasons, she smiled. 'You're in love, aren't you?'

I asked her to swear to secrecy and, having got her word, told her that yes, I was going to see a foreigner I had fallen for although I did not tell her I had slept with him. But she understood my compelling reason to be with my un-named boyfriend because my situation reminded her of a Kurdish-European she had once been seeing covertly before he abandoned her; he could no longer live with the false accusations he had heard about her.

At the end of my narrow street and around the corner, close to a row of small shops, was a taxi stand. I was going to risk taking a cab to David's house, this being a Friday when I knew he would be at home. Areeman said I would be seen by neighbours and if my father found out, well, I could only guess the consequences. But I would only be half an hour—he wouldn't find out.

Even though it was raining and cold, I put on my sunglasses and dressed myself in a long gown over a skirt. My feet, in open-toed sandals, were freezing as I hurried up the street but I was in luck; all the women were indoors with their wood or gas stoves burning on this miserable day and the men were at the mosque. There was one orange and white taxi waiting in the rank. He couldn't believe it when I jumped into the back seat. I had money with me that I had earned from the company. The set rate for anywhere around town was 10 dinars. I told him I would pay him 20 dinars to take me to the UN compound, another 20 for waiting for me, and a further 20 to bring me back.

'*Basha kheshqu* (okay sister).'

So we drove to to the Al-Jamiya district where the UN was located. As we approached the compound the driver told me he didn't want to wait after all, which would be a major problem for me. I wouldn't be able to call up a cab because telephone bookings didn't work and David would not be able to use his driver with the big UN words on the side. I increased the waiting time price to 30 dinars, telling him that he was doing very well for himself and that he would have to make a lot of trips around town to make as much as he was getting from me. He finally agreed.

David was stunned to see me when I walked in through the kitchen as usual. We hugged and kissed—and went straight to his bed. I had intended to give him a piece of my mind when I first arrived for keeping me on tenterhooks when he went to Jordan, but all such thoughts vanished when I looked into his face. He was remorseful, insisting that the Jordan job had even surprised him with its immediacy.

But while I hoped he would lift my spirits about escaping from Kurdistan, there was no such news. He was still working on it. I wanted to ask working on what but let it go. He begged me to linger but I had to leave, assuring him I'd try to see him again the following Friday when, perhaps I added, he might have some good news for me.

'Do you have to leave in such a hurry now? Don't you have another hour before your father arrives home from the mosque?'

'I can't risk it, David.'

The taxi driver had waited, much to my relief. He was staring at the big UN flag and must have been wondering what I was up to. The route to and from David's house entailed driving onto the main highway that cut through the city. I was thinking about David, my thoughts drifting back to those precious minutes with him, as we pulled up at a red light on the highway. It was a notorious light, attracting complaints from drivers because it forced them to stop for a minor, virtually unused side road, and took a long time to change to green. Another vehicle stopped beside us as we sat there. My eyes idly settled on it—a big, black four-wheel drive, similar to many of the vehicles that could be seen around town. But the person behind the wheel was no non-descript driver.

It was my father.

THIRTEEN

How many times had my heart come close to stopping since I'd been in Iraq? If never before, it was happening right then. I slowly positioned myself so most of my back was facing the vehicle beside us and drew my scarf further around my face. If my father were to glance into the cab, would he still recognise me? Would he ask himself where he had seen that scarf before? I would have no answers for him if he were to question me about where I had been. If I remained silent, he would easily get the information from the taxi driver.

'I've just realised I'm running well behind time,' I lied to the taxi driver. 'Just go, please, just go.'

'The light's red.'

'Doesn't matter, just go. I'll pay you more.'

He shot forward as I leaned forward for the taxi's behaviour was certain to attract my father's attention and he would probably try to see who the passenger was. At my constant urging, we raced through the smaller streets until we arrived back at a house close to mine, a property with a high wall that prevented the occupants from looking out into the street. I gave the driver a handful of money, then, with my loose sandals off I ran for the life of me towards our home.

'My God, Latifa, you look like you've seen a ghost,' Areeman said as I burst through the door.

'I have,' I said. 'My father's coming, he's right behind. Please don't say anything.'

I hurried into the bathroom to wash. David had been wearing aftershave. I didn't want my father to smell it.

Khalid arrived home a few minutes after I had settled myself down. I was terrified to even look at him. Just two words repeated themselves in my mind: ya-Allah, ya-Allah—oh God, oh God. He called out my name, twice, loudly. My heart pounced with fear. He'd seen me!

But my father suspected nothing. He had brought fruit, my favourite, green apricots that you eat with salt. Later, when I lay on my bed I thought 'never again'. But how was I to see David? If he found a way out for me, how was he going to convey it?

I tried to understand why he had failed to do such a simple thing as picking up the telephone and calling the Australian Embassy in Baghdad. We all knew war was coming and people were already talking about finding ways of getting out of Iraq beforehand. Perhaps David thought that going through official channels, which would have been flooded with desperate people seeking refugee status, would have been too difficult—that I would have been lost in the crowd. But then, I'd been asking him for months, well before a wave of panic had begun to spread through the country's civilian population. He had told me he was working on projects worth many millions of dollars but that when it was all over, whatever fate lay ahead for Iraq, he could see us meeting up in London and always being together.

David had never talked about his background and I didn't really care to ask, although I did question him one day as to whether he was married. He had been, he told me, but it was a long time ago—his wife had not been able to cope with him being away all the time.

My hoped-for escape that Zana had promised appeared to have evaporated. I had cut links with him. If I had continued with his second mission and completed that successfully, whatever it might have been, something told me he would have then asked me to become involved in another covert activity. So Zana's offer of help had faded and David appeared to be dragging his heels. Why was it so difficult for an Australian girl to go home? Then I gave myself the answer: because I was ensnared in an ancient culture where women, generally, were good for only two things: housework and having babies.

I had heard from a cousin, in a general conversation, how people had been able to escape over the border into Turkey with false passports. With a stolen passport, the photo would be replaced and a machine that someone had got hold of or made would then be used to put a plastic sheen over the picture.

Then I heard that my mother was in town! She had turned up, with my young sister, at her family home, without any notice to me and only to my father, through a message. She made no effort to see me but after much persuasion through my aunties she agreed to meet me. We met in the home of her 'dying' father—who remained fit and well—and my emotions were all over the place. I wanted to both hug her and slap her. I wanted to ask her, over and over, 'why?' But I couldn't ask the question. I could not get that word out. It was apparent from the way she looked at me and from her general conversation with me—'How is your work? Are you studying here yet? If you need warmer clothes I can send you some?—that she had no intention of taking me back with her or of returning my passport. Yet I had clung to every word that she spoke, looking for the tiniest clue that she was pleased with the way I had been living in Dohuk and just might take me back.

Her indifference dismayed me, but it was my father who was most affected. She had come to formalise her divorce from him and to inspect the land that she had arranged for her brothers to have, land bought with my father's hard-earned money from Australia and from the sale of the Sydney house. Almost as soon as she had come, she left. My father allowed his emotions to show only once to me. 'That bitch,' he said.

One day a young man aged in his 20s, who was a friend of a brother of the girls across the road, saw me in their house and said he'd heard I was Baian's daughter. How helpful she had been to an uncle in Germany, he said. And how ironic, I thought, that my mother had a reputation for helping everyone, but she had abandoned her own daughter in Kurdistan, knowing how much I would suffer.

This young man, Rujvan, had opened a fruit-juice shop in Dohuk and I promised to call in there when I was shopping with one of my aunties. On such expeditions I would buy shampoo and body lotions and even a new towel because I always threw out towels and toothbrushes after three or four weeks. I always hoped, too, that when I was in town I would see David walking or driving past. When we eventually called in at the fruit shop I managed, out of earshot of my aunties, to get a word with the man whose uncle had been helped by my mother when I returned our empty cups to him. I had decided to lay all my cards on the table.

'I want to join my mother back in Germany, but I can't get out. I've lost my passport,' I fibbed. 'I've heard it's possible to get another

165

passport. For my mother's sake, do you know how I can get one? Of course, I will take with me any messages to give to your uncle over there in Germany.'

He immediately understood my plight. Keeping his voice low, he said: 'You can get one, but it will cost you $US6000. If war comes, it will be even more.'

'There's no way I can raise that kind of money,' I said, my heart sinking. 'I just need to get into Turkey and from there I could get to the Australian Consulate in Istanbul, or speak to a tourist who could help me through one of their consulates. I just need to get over the border.'

One of my aunties approached from behind me and Rujvan immediately changed the subject to the impending war, an event that was on everyone's lips. I ordered more drinks for us all and told my aunt I would bring them back to the table. That gave me another couple of minutes with Rujvan.

'Do you have gold?'

'Some.' It was what David had given me on return from his overseas trips and the jewellery my mother had sent to me as part of her plan for me to sink into Kurdistan culture. She knew that I only liked silver, but in any case perhaps she had inadvertently provided me with a way out. Rujvan asked me to give him a few days and he'd get back to me, as long as I could get back to the juice shop. That I thought would be fairly easy—getting into a conversation with him again might be more difficult.

My hopes now lay in this third possibility after Zana and David—so far—had failed to come up with any solution. What encouraged me was the knowledge that if one family helped another, the favour had to be returned in one way or another. I hoped that Rujvan, whose name means 'sunlight for all', and particularly for me, perhaps, would feel obliged to do all he could because of my mother's assistance to his uncle. I found ways of calling him from either the house of the girls across the street or from another cousin's home—which had a separate line upstairs—when I visited them with my aunties.

A week of surreptitious phone calls later I could not believe my ears.

'I have good news,' said Rujvan. 'I have found a way for you to not only get across the border into Turkey but all the way to Istanbul. But do you have $US6000 worth of gold? Without it being paid up front, they won't take you.'

'I don't know the exact value, but at an estimate I would say that putting everything I have together, it would be worth much more than that.'

I asked for more details. Although I was excited about escaping, I had heard of refugees, asylum seekers, whatever you cared to call them, suffocating to death in crowded trucks on the way to Germany. I asked him about the transport.

'There's just one other family involved. There will be a small bus on the Turkish side that will take you all the way to Istanbul. They'll provide you with accommodation on the way because it's going to take four or five days to get there from the border.'

I pressed him for more details. If he had the answers, I would believe what he was telling me. If he 'ummed' and 'ahhed' I would have my doubts. He did not hesitate. I would be taken there at a time when the frontier was closed during the afternoon and the guards were 'off duty'. Anything they collected, money-wise, during their official siesta period, would go straight into their pockets. I asked how he knew so much and he revealed that he had been involved in getting several other families out of Kurdistan. I did not even think what a curious thing it was that I should have found a possible way out during a conversation with a man who ran a juice bar.

We planned my escape to coincide with a religious festival, when the city would be alive with people coming and going, calling at relatives' homes. To make things even easier, I had managed to persuade my father to let me stay with one of his sisters, who was entertaining many of her other relatives. The house was crowded with a large number of adults and no less than 35 children. I had left my father's house looking 'normal' with just a small overnight bag, but inside I had packed my gold jewellery, a skirt and black boots. Then, from my aunty's house I was able to slip away on the pretext of calling on a mutual friend across the road. The festival gave me that small window of freedom and fortunately nobody took any notice of me leaving with the small bag.

I hurried up a steep hill to where I saw the navy blue BMW that Rujvan said he would be driving. It was a 1997 model, he was to explain, relatively new for Iraq. My heart was pounding with excitement as I reached for the rear door handle. I just knew I could trust him. As I clambered into the back seat he turned back and grinned. 'Within a few hours you'll be free,' he said. Rujvan was dressed in a black jeans jacket with a white shirt underneath, his hair neatly groomed as though this was a special occasion for him, too.

I wanted to kiss the back of his neck, but held myself back. 'You haven't even left Dohuk yet, girl!' I told myself.

'We won't even have to stop anywhere. We have a full tank of gas.'

We headed north across the desert plains, parts of which were white with a blanket of snow. The roads were slippery so Rujvan kept his speed down. I wanted to urge him on, terrified that I was already being missed and people were out looking for me. But with each passing kilometre my confidence grew. I checked my watch. It was shortly after 11.15am. We'd been driving for more than an hour. Zakho, our frontier destination, would now be less than half an hour away. I reached down through my clothes, just to make sure the jewellery was there. That was all I needed. Just some spare clothes and the payment for my passage out of there. I was trying to imagine how it would be back at my crowded aunty's house. Perhaps someone was already asking: 'Where's Latifa? I haven't seen her for a while.'

Then someone else would say: 'She's gone to see a friend. She should be back soon.'

Well, I wouldn't be. Not this time.

I asked Rujvan about the other family he had mentioned, the one who also wanted to leave. He said they had been moved a few days earlier because the authorities had heard whispers about their plans.

'Did they get away?' I asked.

He laughed. 'Well, they didn't come back so they must have.'

We did stop once, for a toilet break at a garage in a village, before pressing on to our destination.

Zakho was a poor frontier town whose 350,000 inhabitants suffered from the winter snows. Everything was closed down. People shut their doors and tried to stay warm. We wound through the largely deserted streets until Rujvan began to slow as we approached a grey box-like house that stood apart from the cluster of other buildings. A smaller structure attached to the house appeared to be full of first-aid materials, with red crosses on the containers and rolls of bandages. Rujvan told me to wait in the car while he went inside.

I had no idea what this building was, or who Rujvan was speaking to. I forced myself to have only positive thoughts. I was getting away! I didn't even care how much hardship awaited me on the Turkish side of the border, just as long as I found myself on a bus heading for Istanbul.

He was inside for 15 minutes before returning to the car. 'Latifa, give me your jewellery,' he said. 'He wants to weigh it.'

So I gave him a smaller bag containing my rings, necklaces and bracelets. I felt a tinge of sadness, for among the collection were pieces that David had given me. I'd also brought all the money I had, 3000 dinars, which was about $US250, but I wasn't going to part with that, believing that I would need some cash for the journey across Turkey. I'd considered trying to exchange it for US dollars or Turkish money in the city before leaving but, aside from seizing the chance to break away from my aunties during a shopping expedition, I would have drawn very serious attention to myself—a single woman approaching a money changer and asking for American dollars.

They were taking a long time. What were they doing in there?

It was a good half an hour before Rujvan stepped out through the door. His expression alarmed me and I jumped from the vehicle.

'What's wrong, Rujvan?'

He lowered his head. Then he raised his eyes to mine.

'He says it's not enough.'

'But it's worth more than $6000. I've already told you that.'

'He says $6000 is for passports. This is a special job, getting you across the border without a passport.'

No, no, no. I couldn't believe this.

A man had stepped out from the building and had propped himself against the doorway. In his 50s and balding, he wore a stained, white shirt and dusty black pants held up by a leather and chrome belt, a grey-black stubble around his chin and a thick moustache. He looked like the Turkmani that he was, but he could have stepped out of a B-grade Western movie, playing the bad guy. He had crossed one leg in front of the other and was drawing on a cigarette, puffing smoke into the air as he looked at a point beyond me. Strangely, I noticed that his boots were shiny black as though he had just polished them.

'I've got an extra $US250,' I cried. 'Tell him I'll give him that. It's all I have. I'll worry about any other needs when I get into Turkey.'

Rujvan grimaced and went back to the man. I saw the stranger shaking his head.

When Rujvan returned I started to head towards the doorway, but he stopped me.

'Just let me talk to him,' I said. 'Let me explain my plight—that having come here I have left my home and I've put my life in great danger.'

'He's a Turkmani, don't forget. He won't understand your dialect. I can only just get by with him.'

'Please, please, Rujvan, try again. There has to be a way.'

The man was still smoking, still gazing nonchalantly into the distance. To think that my life probably hung on a decision that this ugly character would now make as Rujvan walked back to him.

This time, as I paced up and down beside the BMW, watching the two men, I saw no shaking of heads. But Rujvan's head was low once more as he returned to me.

'Tell me,' I said, desperation in my voice.

'Sister, I don't know how I can tell you. May God forgive me.'

'What are you saying, Rujvan? Tell me, for heaven's sake!'

'Sister, I am ashamed to say this. But there is another way as well as paying the gold.'

'Yes, he wants all my money. He can have it.'

Rujvan lowered his face from mine. 'No, he wants you. He wants you to be his all the way through the journey. *Staferlallah*—God forgive me—for telling you this.'

'What are you talking about? Are you saying—'

'Yes, you have to give yourself to him.'

'You mean sleep with him.'

'He says you have not brought enough gold or money and this is the only way.'

'Sleep with that man over there day and night, whenever he asks, all the way through to Istanbul?'

Rujvan kept his head down. The man in the door continued smoking.

'You have used me, Rujvan. You knew this was going to happen, didn't you?'

My voice was trembling. I wanted to kill him. But perhaps he didn't know. He seemed genuinely remorseful. I glared at the man in the doorway who had finally turned his eyes towards me, watching for my reaction.

'Rujvan, go back to that man and tell him that if he wants to fuck someone, he can fuck himself. Then come back to me, start up your car and get me back to Dohuk as fast as you can. Every minute lost now is a minute closer to a punishment that I cannot imagine.'

As Rujvan made to turn back towards the house I grabbed his arm. 'Don't bother—we have already lost precious time.'

As we sped back along potholed roads, my gold and my money back in my bag, all I heard was Rujvan's apologies and his pleas for forgiveness. I didn't know whether to believe him or not. But one thing I was certain of—if I had set out on the road with that villainous character I had just come face to face with, I had no doubt that he would have had his way with me and dumped me at the roadside with a slit throat. I looked at my watch. By the time we got back to my aunty's house, we would have been away for more than four hours. Dusk would be approaching. Too long to have been absent. Far too long.

'Please drive faster,' I told Rujvan, but he was already travelling at a frightening pace around bends.

And then, in the middle of nowhere, the car broke down.

FOURTEEN

We drifted to the side of the road, the engine silent. Rujvan turned the key, time and again, but the car was dead. He tapped the fuel gauge, revealing to me that he didn't know much about car engines, then got out and opened the bonnet. Wind swept through the valley but that was the only thing that moved. There wasn't another car to be seen.

I sat inside, numb.

Rujvan came to the window. 'I've checked the wires and they are all okay and there is water. I cannot understand what the problem is.'

I didn't care about his stupid car, although I should have, because it had to get me home. But I did not want to hear what was working and what wasn't—I just wanted to hear it start.

'Don't you have a mobile phone?' I said, getting out of the vehicle. 'Can't you call a village or somebody and get them to come and help us?'

'Who should I call? I don't know anybody who lives in these parts. Besides, look, there's no signal out here.' He held up the phone towards me. A broken down car and a useless phone. Worse, a failed attempt to escape and I didn't know how I was going to explain my absence if I ever got out of this place.

Fear was spreading through me like wildfire. For a terrible moment I wanted to throw myself off the edge of a cliff, just to escape this terrible predicament. But I suddenly remembered that suicide was a sin. Upset my family, perhaps, but do not upset God. To jump would condemn me to Hell.

'We could try pushing to see if it will start,' said Rujvan, his voice almost lost in the wind, but it was strong enough to bring me back to reality. So I got behind the car and Rujvan positioned himself beside it so he could steer and then jump in. But it was hopeless. I didn't have the strength to push the car out of roadside rut it had stopped in. All seemed lost—when from around a bend behind us came a teenager on a donkey cart, laden down with scrap metal.

Rujvan asked him to stop and help push and at first it looked like he was going to ignore us, but then he stopped the cart and came over to look at the engine. He told Rujvan that his father was a mechanic and he had learned a little bit from him.

'Where is your father?' I asked urgently. 'Is he nearby? Can you ask him to come and help us?'

'My father is dead. He died last year. But he told me things about cars.'

He spent precious minutes—15 perhaps—doing something under the bonnet then he asked Rujvan to try starting the car. The engine coughed and burst into life. I almost burst into tears with happiness. I gave the boy a handful of dinars and asked him what he had done. He mentioned something about rotten wiring and he had put two parts together but we had to be careful not to hit any bumps because they would come apart. All the wiring, he said, looked very, very bad. So much for Rujvan's 'almost new' BMW. He was a typical Kurdish spoiled 'rich boy', caring more for the appearance of the car than the condition of the engine. As is the norm, the look was more important than anything else.

Each time we hit a pothole as we sped on towards Dohuk I prayed the engine would not cut out. Darkness was on us when I reached the street where my father's house was located. I had decided to go straight there, rather than to the home of the aunty I had been at when I had broken away earlier that day. I asked Rujvan to drop me at the top of the hill. Hardly a word had passed between us since the breakdown apart from his occasional mutterings of sorrow about what had happened. I didn't thank him. I just got out.

Down the hill, outside my father's house, I could see a cluster of people—and as I approached them I could see they were my aunties and cousins along with my grandmother. Suddenly a little figure ran towards me—my five-year-old cousin, Yasmin. She knew I was in trouble and took my hand. I could not see my father's car, which meant he wasn't home. I prayed he wasn't out looking for me. Before I reached the house, Shilan, from across the street, ran to me to warn me that everybody had been out looking for me.

'Tell them you were visiting one of my friends,' she said. 'I'll back you up.'

I smiled at her. 'I've been weak enough. I'm going to tough this one out.'

I pushed my way determinedly through the crowd of relatives. If looks could kill, the scowl on my grandmother's face would have sent me to an early grave. I entered the house and made straight for my bedroom. If I thought I would find peace and quiet there I was mistaken. The women burst in through the door and demanded to know where I had been.

'Tell us! Tell us!' came their voices, like a chorus of witches. One of them prodded me in the shoulder. 'Tell us! Tell us!'

That was it. I snapped. I leaped to my feet and screamed at them.

'Get out of my room, you ugly bitches. I've had enough of all of you and your stupid evil ways. Leave me alone.'

There was a tea cup and saucer in the room and I picked it up and hurled it against the wall. The shattered pieces dropped at their feet. One of them started crying, but I had lost it. 'You are the devil's children the way you have been treating me since I arrived. Do this, do that! Who the hell do you think you all are to boss me around? I can't imagine how your husbands can even lie with you. You all have the devil's horns beneath those veils. I'm an adult and I'm an Australian so piss off out of my room!'

How do you silence a coven of witches? You give them a taste of their own medicine, that's how. They were all silent.

Then I went for them, pushing them back out through the door. 'Get out of my bedroom, you ugly whores, you home wreckers.'

I slammed the door on them. I could hear them talking about me on the other side, but I didn't care. Shaking uncontrollably, I lay down on the bed and tried to sleep.

A knocking on the bedroom door roused me the next morning. Then one of my aunties put her head around the door, and, as though nothing had happened the previous night, asked: 'Aren't you coming out to eat, to survive?'

My mood had not changed. 'The same old shit? I'll get my own breakfast, thank you.'

I made my way out to the kitchen and cut some fruit and ate it with bread and cheese. Then I defiantly went to the men's room and sat down and watched TV. My grandmother just looked at me, her face a grey shade of white. My father had stayed away overnight visiting a relative out of town and when he arrived home he appeared perfectly normal. I knew then that he had heard nothing of the events of the day before. I couldn't face being in that house with either him or particularly his mother, because I feared a storm was gathering over my head and I needed space to build up my inner resources. I asked if I could stay at the home of his elder sister, my Aunt Khalida for a day or two, seeing that I had no job to go to.

When I arrived at her home, she also tried to pretend that nothing had happened the day before. But in the bedroom one of my female cousins, who had witnessed my performance, asked: 'What happened to you, Latifa? It is like you were possessed by the devil.'

I smiled at her, for being younger than me, she did not deserve my wrath. My father, who had brought me to the house, stayed there for dinner and then returned to his home. But when he got there, I was to learn later from a relative he repeated the events to, that my grandmother asked him: 'Where is your daughter?'

He told her he had left me at Khalida's home, to which my grandmother replied: 'You had better go straight back over there and get her or she will run away again, like she did yesterday.'

I do not know whether Rujvan had told friends or relatives that he had taken me to the border—although I doubt it because he would have received a severe punishment—but just hearing that I had 'run away' was enough for my father.

An hour after he had left Khalida's home he was back again, banging on the door. I was at the bedroom door when I heard Khalida say:

'Oh, you're back—did you forget something?'

'Did I forget something? Yes, I forgot something. I forgot to kill my daughter.'

He stormed through the house, carrying a thick piece of electrical cable, 2.5 centimetres in diameter and 1 metre long. I retreated back into the bedroom and fell down on the bed and then he was on me. He raised his arm and brought the cable down hard and fast across my thigh. The burning hot pain was so intense I could not even find a voice to scream. Then the cable came down again, and again, across my legs and my arms that I had thrown up around my head for protection. In a momentary glance I saw the venom on his face, the utter hatred. It was only the intervention of Khalida's husband, Abdul Salam, who had rushed out of the shower room on hearing his wife screaming with fear for me, that prevented my father continuing to beat the life out of me. With a monumental effort, Abdul Salam managed to pull my father, wild with uncontrolled rage, away from me and out of the room. Blood began to soak through my *dijasha* from the wounds that had been inflicted through the material. I felt as though my body was dangling in fire. Yet I had not uttered a word, not unleashed as much as a whimper. I knew I was in shock, for my body was trembling violently from head to toe. They say that your whole life passes before you when you are dying. I don't really know how close I had come—for at what point does a heart stop when the body can take no more pain?—but what I do know is that as those vicious blows rained down on me I saw the faces of my little sister Bojeen and David, the man I loved so deeply. I even felt his warm kiss, but it was really only the blood on my lips.

Khalid demanded that I return home with him that night but Abdul said I would be too weak to travel after the beating he had given me. What shocked me as much as the attack was the fact that he had not even asked me for an explanation for my absence. It was enough for him to hear from my grandmother that I had 'run away'. What my father's savagery had revealed to me was the fatal punishment I could expect should he ever discover that I was not a virgin. If he could do that to me for running away, I had no doubt what he would do were he to discover my 'secret'.

As a female cousin helped me towards the bathroom to bathe my wounds, I fell backwards in a faint. She had to guide me to the bed, but not before I heard my father, who had been made to sit on a sofa, tell AbdulSalam: 'She is just like her mother. Deceitful and wicked.' Then the curses, mixed with my name, fell from his lips. I had never heard him use such language. Oh, how he must have hated me. And there it was again—'just like her mother'. His own mother used that comparison and he had learned her words well.

My head was spinning as my cousin washed my wounds with a bucket of hot water she had brought in. Black bruises were appearing beside the red gashes where the skin had torn. Outside the door I could hear my father and AbdulSalam arguing. AbdulSalam was actually taking my side.

'It's all your fault, brother. If you had never taken your wife and your children to Australia none of this would have happened. You were all happy here. Your daughter would have grown up and married and by now you would be a grandfather. You've thrown your life away and the lives of your children.'

I did not hear my father's response for a wave of dizziness came over me. Now the pain from the wounds was unbearable, like someone was dragging red hot wires across my flesh. Of course, my father had had no choice but to flee Kurdistan 20 years earlier or we would have all been hunted down and killed anyway.

'You must calm down, Khalid,' said AbdulSalam. 'There must have been a good reason why she wanted to run away.'

Then I heard my father speak out. 'I have done everything possible to teach the values of Islam. I buy her favourite foods, she still refused to go to university and I still allow her to wear pants. And yes, I'm as angry with her mother as I am with her. What kind of family is this to have brought such wickedness upon me?'

Aunty Khalida came into the room to check on me. When she saw the wounds, her jaw dropped in shock.

'You know what you must do, to prevent him attacking you again—you must go out there and kiss his hands or his feet and beg for his forgiveness.'

I couldn't believe what she was saying. My father had beaten me within an inch of my life and now she wanted me to apologise to him?

'I'm not going out there. I won't say sorry. I've done nothing wrong. If I had committed a crime or a terrible sin, I would accept his beating. But simply wanting to get away from a prison that has been built around me, for no reason whatsoever, is not what I consider wrongdoing. No, Aunty Khalida, I won't apologise.'

'Come out with me,' she said, making for the door. 'It's the only way.'

I refused to follow her. So she came back in and begged me, for the sake of the whole family, to apologise and clear the air. To leave this rift between me and my father unsettled would leave me open to further attack and the family would rest uneasily in their beds, uncertain what he would do next.

She spoke to me for a good 30 minutes, holding my hands, beseeching me to go out to my father. 'Lose your pride, Latifa. If you do not say sorry to him, you'll give him the impression that you believe you were in the right to run away. Apologise, please, for all of us, or he will carry his anger with him everywhere he goes.'

She put up a convincing argument and finally I relented. She helped me to my feet, for the wounds on my legs stung so when I tried to move. Like a cripple, I limped out through the door. My father was sitting on a couch. I sat on the other end, my shaking hands in my lap, putting as much distance between him and me as I could. He would not even look at me. He sat very still, glaring at the carpet, his lips tight. For several minutes we remained like that. My aunt whispered something to her husband, then AbdulSalam walked over to me, knelt beside me and said softly: 'Isn't there something you are supposed to say now? Something you are supposed to do?'

It was one of the hardest things I had ever had to do—not just rise up, unassisted, from the couch but then approach the man who had inflicted these injuries upon me. I stood in front of him, then, with equal effort, lowered myself to my knees in front of him. I took each of his hands in mine, leaned forward and kissed them, then I brought them up to my forehead.

'I'm sorry,' I said. 'Please forgive me.'

He snatched his hands from mine. I lowered my face and kissed his bare foot and begged again for his forgiveness.

He raised his foot and shoved me away. The vicious thrust sent me sprawling onto my back. I looked up to see the face of my aunt staring down at me as she shook her head. I saw in her expression that there was no hope of winning my father's forgiveness, let alone his blessing.

I pulled myself up and walked slowly to my room and now the tears were flowing. I heard my aunty say: 'You must let her stay here until she's ready to go home. I don't think after any of this she'll run away again.'

'She will die, without question, if she does,' I heard my father say deliberately. 'One more event, no matter what it is, that brings shame to me or this family, and I will kill her.'

The silence that followed in that room left me in no doubt that those relatives who heard the threat knew that he meant every word.

Lying on the bed, my thoughts went back over the risks I had taken. Even turning down marriage proposals as they had come in was a risk, for I believed that my grandmother in particular was growing more and more suspicious each time I sent one of the calling mothers away. She had asked me more than once why I had refused handsome, wealthy suitors, men who other girls would have fallen over one another to have as a husband. I had always replied that until I knew someone well and fell in love with them—a word I dared to suggest meant nothing to her—I would continue to turn down the offers. She and my father, I knew, would not allow my attitude to continue and one day they would drag me off to the Imam.

Such scenarios did exist. A woman I had met at a wedding, a very pleasant girl several years older than me, had been paired off with a cousin and although she liked him, she was terrified of the time when she would be married off and would have to have sex. The thought of it frightened her so much that after managing to keep her husband at bay on the wedding night, she ran away to the home of a compassionate relative. They tracked her down there, dragged her back to the husband's home and literally bound her, spreadeagled to the bed. Her screams, I learned, echoed through the house and into the street, before the husband emerged, victorious. An inspection of the sheets told his relatives that he was indeed a man.

Memories of the other risks I had taken swept over me. Aside from the actual act of having my virginity cruelly taken from me, there had been my affair with David, right under the noses of people who would have supported my father in whatever punishment he handed out to me. I shuddered at the narrow escape I'd had when his jeep and my taxi were stopped side by side at that traffic light.

My father still did not know just how serious my escape attempt had been on that desperate flight to the border. All he knew was that I had 'run away' when I had gone missing. Would he have taken a gun or a knife to me if he'd known I had been ready to hand over all the gold jewellery and money I had to cross the frontier?

It's always the woman who is to blame for any 'indiscretion'.

One day, not long after I had arrived in Dohuk, I had needed some treatment for an aching tooth and my father arranged for me to see a dentist who was a relative. Like my aunty's husband in Baghdad, the man was a letcher. As I was lying back in his chair, he thrust himself hard up against my thigh. Then he gripped me from behind, his hands part way on my breasts as he helped me into a sitting position. I knew exactly what he was up to but rather than confront him I asked my father if next time I could go to a different dentist because I was not happy with my 'treatment'—in more ways than one. My father refused, saying: 'Always support your relatives. Never give business to outsiders.' I never went back and fortunately my toothache went away.

My thoughts, as I lay in my aunty's room, drifted to my cousin Etab, the victim of the honour killing. That poor girl had been forced into marriage at 14 and had her first child at 15. While my mother had told me the story when I was in my early teens in Australia, the terrible details were relayed to me in Dohuk by my Aunt Khalida, in whose house I now lay after the beating from my father. Etab's husband, like my own father, had been a freedom fighter who was often away but because she was so often alone, rumours began to sweep the town that she was taking advantage of his absence to have affairs. Fearing for her life and that of her three children, she managed to escape into Iraq, but her husband—her first cousin and a relative of my father—was eventually able to contact her and persuade her to come back.

That very first night of her return, she was woken by her father and father-in-law in the early hours of the morning. They wanted her to help them pick fruit and vegetables on land they owned. Etab knew this was the end. Because her own mother and grandmother had been slaughtered and she knew one day it would be her turn, no matter how innocent and worthy she was. She was her mother's daughter. She gave her children a kiss and slipped her gold bracelet on her eldest daughter's wrist. There were a group of men sitting in the back of the Toyota truck. As they sped past the vegetable garden and on into the desert, Etab prayed to Allah that it would be quick. But it wasn't.

Like a cave woman, she was dragged by her hair from the vehicle by her father and petrol was poured over her as she knelt in fear. Her father struck a match and threw it on her and as her screams rang out, he brought out a gun and fired a number of bullets into her body. The burned and bullet-riddled corpse was found later that day and although the police had by law to put an appeal in the local newspaper for any witnesses or anyone who could identify the victim, no-one came forward. It couldn't have been Etab, everyone said, because surely, she was in Iran. . . ? As for Etab's children, the eldest now being 13, the next eight and the youngest five, the two oldest had been forced into early slavery by their father's family.

How do I know this? Because one of my aunties took me around to the house for a visit and I saw the pitiful sight of the youngest girl washing men's trousers while the older one was scrubbing the kitchen floor. It was as though they were being punished for the 'sins' of their mother.

I was so sorry for their plight that I was able to persuade my aunty to take me back there on a couple of occasions, when I took along candies, hairpins, books and pencils for the girls. My heart bled to see them in filthy *dijashas* as they went about their washing chores so the adults could wear nice clean clothes and live in a spotless house.

One day I asked the girls' grandmother: 'Why do you make them work so hard when they are so young?'

She snapped back at me. 'Because that's the way they are being trained.'

Before I could stop myself, I said: 'Why don't you just kill them now, like their poor mother? Because you will eventually.'

The grandmother later told my aunty what I had said and my aunty in turn told my father. He had slapped me across the face. 'Don't ever interfere in other people's business,' he ordered.

The night of my punishment with the cable, I cried into my pillow not only for my own throbbing wounds, but for Etab and all the other women in this wretched place who had suffered so. This culture was so barbaric. But how was it ever to change when every time a woman dared to answer back or try to escape she was severely punished or killed?

It had been arranged that I would stay with my Aunt Khalida for two or three days while I recovered and then my father would return for me. But he came back the following evening, ordering me to pack my clothes—the clothes I had hoped to be wearing by now as I travelled by bus towards Istanbul and freedom. My aunt Areeman, who had called by, was surprised at my father's earlier-than-expected return. I feared the worst. He had come for me when it was dark, just as they had once come for Etab.

I wanted to turn to my cousins and tell them: 'If anything happens to me, just remember these words—All I wanted to do was go home.' But I stopped myself from saying it, even though I believed as I left with my stern-faced father that I was a dead woman walking.

My aunties and a number of other cousins came to the door to watch me climb into my father's jeep, as though it was a farewell forever. My father, who had suddenly taken up smoking, drew heavily on his Marlboro cigarette as he turned to look at them, but he said nothing. All I could think about as we headed home was the route he was taking. I knew the directions well and I feared that if he diverted, it could be a sign of impending doom. Although he said nothing, I could sense his rage. What had happened to him? Had the death of his brother in that car crash affected him? Or was it living with that mother of his? Perhaps, though, he had just sunk back into a culture that I never knew, having been carried through the mountains, away from it, when I was only two.

My grandmother was in her room when we arrived back at the house and I went straight to my prison, my bedroom. Having eaten very little in the past two days, I rose for breakfast the following morning to join my father and his mother, slouched in her usual way, all in black, on a cushion on the floor. None of us spoke until, towards the end of the meal, my father's harsh voice broke the silence as his mother turned her eyes towards me as though she wanted to add emphasis to his words.

'From this moment on, you will not be permitted to set foot out of this house without my permission. You will wash the dishes, the morning dishes, the lunch dishes and the evening dishes. You will not allow your grandmother to present the food for any guests, you will not allow her to do any sweeping and you will obey her every command. You will keep this house in perfect order.'

There was no point in fighting him. I turned my head towards him, making sure I ignored my grandmother who I knew in my heart had discussed all this with him. She had been engaged to my paternal grandfather when she was nine and had married him at the age of 13, entering a miserable life of slavery and childbirth. No wonder she wanted someone—me—to take over the household duties.

'Basch,—okay—I will do as you wish,' I told my father. I had spoken in Arabic, which I had quickly picked up, rather than the English I had occasionally used with my father or the local Baideeni dialect. My grandmother had grown up in Mosul, an Arab town, so she understood exactly when I had agreed to the humiliating rules my father had just imposed. There was a glint of satisfaction in her eyes.

I immediately began picking up the breakfast dishes and taking them out into the kitchen. When I returned to the living room to pick up the remainder, my father said: 'There is one other thing. You will start to pray. You will pray every day like me and your grandmother.'

'I don't even know how to pray. It's not something I have grown up with.' I wanted to add: 'I grew up with you in Australia, remember—you who smoked and drank all day.' But I kept my mouth shut.

His intention to show me how to pray left me with a feeling of unease. It would be another victory over my perceived insolence. So when they were both out one day I put my life in my hands and hurried across the street to my friends. I asked the girls to teach me how to pray, telling myself that perhaps this might be to my advantage, that the God I had never learned to love might help me. They showed me in which direction I should stand and kneel, how to bow and they wrote everything down for me as they spoke, including the essential verses from the Koran.

When my father returned from work that day I told him that I had recalled from my cousins in Germany how to pray and I was now ready to do it. A flicker of a smile crossed his face. He told me that it was already time to go to my room and start my *mughrib* (sunset prayers). He gave me a prayer mat and in my room I positioned it to face east, using the plan the girls had drawn for me, showing me how my bedroom was positioned in relation to Mecca. The evening prayer is shorter than those chanted during the day, but I made sure my father could hear me, having left the bedroom door slightly ajar.

How strange, I told myself, that praying started to grow on me. I prayed in the morning and took time throughout the day to go into my room and repeat the verses from the Koran. I became interested in the stories of the prophets, as related in the Koran, the book my father had given me with its translations and pronounciations. What came to me was the knowledge that God was all knowing and as the weeks went by, with my routine of cleaning and praying, I began to feel more at peace. Not an entire peace, because I was aware that my father was watching my every move and that led me on to thinking about the plight of women generally in that country.

When my aunt from Baghdad visited us, I enjoyed talking to her about some of the meanings in the Koran. She told me she hoped I understood that the Koran told of how important it was for a woman to dress modestly and that—despite my interjections—a man and a woman are equal in the eyes of God. In between these devout conversations, her lecherous husband was still taking every advantage to touch me. On one occasion, when I was sitting on the stool in the washroom, taking my 'shower', I caught him staring down at me over the top of a dividing wall, that did not quite reach the ceiling. He had snuck into a storage room next to the wash room and had clambered onto sacks of rice to look down on me.

I quickly called out to my aunty, asking if she could come right away and help me wash my back. I heard a panicky scrambling in the store room as he sought out a hiding place before she arrived. I made sure that didn't happen again—I secured a large piece of cardboard over the gap. My reasons for not revealing his perversions were simply that it would cause enormous trouble and I had no doubt my father would turn his wrath onto me yet again.

Women were without doubt nothing but sex objects in the eyes of a Kurdish man. They were good only for making babies and working like slaves for the family. The Islamic Hadith (a book of teaching) states that a woman should satisfy a man's every sexual need, which is very strong.

I settled down into doing the housework. I was subtly, so subtly I didn't realise it, turning from a free-spirited woman of the West to

189

a 'converted' slave of the Middle East. Cleaning, praying, cleaning, praying. I would have been swallowed up in that daily routine and become deeply engulfed in a culture that had consumed every woman in the cities, the valley communities and the mountain villages for hundreds of kilometres around had my body not resisted.

My hair began to fall out in handfuls.

FIFTEEN

'Khoulisar—your hair!' cried my cousin Areeman as she was plaiting my long black locks one morning. Khoulisar is a name my cousins sometimes used for me, for it literally means a person who has gone from one problem to another, like someone going from the frying pan to the fire. 'You've got big bald patches here at the back.'

I had noticed hair loss when I was showering, but thought nothing of it. Now as I reached around I felt my smooth scalp.

'What does it mean?' I cried. 'Have I got cancer?'

Areeman suggested consulting a relative, one of my father's sisters, who had studied medicine, but who had given up because she couldn't stand the sight of blood. When she called at the house she shook her head; my condition was a mystery to her. She told my father that I should see a doctor and after a hesitation—why he had to hestitate upset me—he agreed to drive me to a doctor, accompanied by Areeman and an aunt. The GP turned out to be a male, but as the consultation was about hair, rather than personal women's business, there was no problem in allowing him to touch me. The waiting room was full of women sitting with their obviously sick children, who were coughing and wheezing. I felt so sorry for them.

The doctor quickly picked that I was a 'foreign Kurd' and when I told him I was from Australia he smiled. 'Ah, the land of kangaroos. And is it true you see them in the street?'

'Some places,' I said, thinking of outback towns where occasionally a stray animal will bound down the road. He had relatives in Australia and his general conversation put me at ease. Finally, touching my bare scalp, he said: 'This is *nafcia*—depression. Do you find you are sleeping a lot?'

'When she's not doing the housework she's always sleeping,' my aunt ventured.

'And do you feel very tired all the time?'

'All the time,' I said.

'Well, there's no direct cure for this. But if it gives you any confidence we can take a blood test. The alternative is to pray to Allah.'

'We'll pray,' said my aunt. 'Allah gave her this pain and he will take it from her when the time is right.'

Rather than suggest a cure or give me any hope, the doctor had only added to my depression. My father, who had been waiting outside, asked what the doctor had said and on hearing that I was 'stressed and feeling down' he retorted: 'Why is she feeling stressed? She is fed well, she has her own room. She is better off than many people.'

I sat in the rear seat for the drive home, staring out of the window, looking at nothing. My concerns about my hair appeared to add

Above: My grandmother. Right: My father in his garden, listening to news about the US invasion of Iraq.

Top: Me and my cousin from Texas, Vahel, who came to Dohuk as an interpreter with the US military.
Above: My father, in white, with his new wife Jamilla, at a cousin's wedding. I am second from the left.

Top: Me with my friend Shilan as we prepare for her engagement party. Above: On one of my mother's visits to Dohuk with my sister Bojeen, we went to a juice bar with my aunt Vian. On this occasion, like others, I pleaded in vain for my mother to take me out of Kurdistan

Bottom: I accompanied two of the Americans as an interpreter to a barbecue in the hills, where we were greeted by the village chief.
Below: My friends the Americans outside the compound in Dohuk, where I worked.

Top: At a work barbecue—the soldiers were never without their weapons, even while they ate.
Above: One day I accompanied one of the soldiers into town to interpret as he shopped for rugs.

Top: Kurdish soldiers working for the US military.
Above: Free-almost! Waiting in a Baghdad hotel on my way home, still shocked by my experience.

Top: The aircraft that flew me out of Mosul. Above: A fond momento photo of me and one of the US soldiers who was so kind to me.

Top: On my way home to Australia, I was met by an Australian diplomatic official during a stop-over in the Gulf.

Above: The weddings continue. A recent photo of my cousin Vasheen's wedding—and his 14-year old bride. My mother is second from the right.

to the problem for I now noticed it coming out in handfuls in the bathroom. I began wearing the *hijab* in the house. Perhaps this was God's way of forcing me to obey the life of a true Muslim woman, I told myself wryly.

While it had become extremely risky to run across the road to my neighbours—which meant I couldn't call David, whose voice would have cheered me and helped me get over my depression—the girls were allowed to come and see me. They tried to time it for occasions when my father was at work and my grandmother was at the shops or sleeping. They did not enjoy being in her company. Their visits were the only bright moments in my life. We would share photographs and clip our nails, although painting them was out. Deep down, though, my depression lingered—and was soon to manifest itself in another dramatic way.

When I woke one morning and went to the mirror to check on the state of my hair I reeled back in shock. My face was covered in red spots. They were all over my body, twice the size of pimples, but they did not itch. I had to wait patiently around the house, going about my chores as though nothing had happened, until my aunt arrived. It was in order for me to travel to the doctor with my aunt, because she was a married adult. I had covered my face, such an embarrassment, with the scarf so that only my eyes showed. People who saw me passing by in the car might have thought: 'There's a devout woman.'

This time the doctor, baffled by my condition, insisted on taking a blood test, suggesting at the same time that not only was I depressed but I might also be lacking iron or vitamins. He said I should continue praying to Allah. I wondered whether he really knew what he was doing—particularly when, the following morning, I woke to find that the right side of my face had swollen up like a balloon. I looked a sight—balding, spotty and swollen faced.

Studying the results of the blood test later, the doctor told me I was generally healthy but I was not getting enough sunlight. That much I knew.

'What I would do is try to get more sun and—'

'. . . pray to Allah.'

He gave me a look, but I was at the end of my tether.

The communication between my Aunt Hadar in Baghdad and my father was through the phone at my neighbours' house. One of the girls would run across the road and tell my father there was a call for him and when the next opportunity came to speak to her, my father told her of my condition. Listening to the symptoms, she agreed with the doctor's initial assessment—*nafcia*.

She made the long journey from Baghdad, without her sleazy husband this time, in the hope of bringing me some comfort and while it was lovely to see her, there wasn't much she could do. Unless she could persuade my father to at least allow me get out and about she feared my condition would not only remain but get worse. Despite my cynicism, I had also been asking Allah during my daily prayers to make me better. I had by now fallen into a regular prayerful routine and while I had begun merely to quell my father's anger I soon gained great comfort from falling to my knees on the mat in my bedroom. So far, my prayers had remained unanswered.

'We've been discussing your problem,' my father told me one day as I brought the food out while my aunt was still staying with us. 'We will take you to the pond where the water will do you a lot of good.'

I had heard of this special pond. It had a reputation like Lourdes in France, where the sick gathered to be healed. In a small way, the pond was said to have brought good health to the ailing but I remained sceptical. For a start, as it was winter and bitterly cold. Although the sun was shining, the water would be unbearable.

'You have nothing to lose,' said my aunt.

So we drove for 20 minutes to the lake, which was fed by pure water from the surrounding mountains. A cruel wind swept across the plains and I had to force myself to step out of my father's jeep. I was wearing a thick tracksuit with a dijasha over the top and at the urging of my father and aunt I jumped in—fully clothed, of course, in case there were prying eyes. The icy water, reaching up to my chest, took my breath away.

'Wash your hair, bathe your face!' they cried from the bank.

I did as I was told and then clambered back, shivering uncontrollably as my father threw a blanket over my wet clothes while my aunt got dry clothes out of the car and then held up a large sheet as I changed. I was still trembling when we arrived back. I needed a hot shower and then had to sit beside a small oil heater in my bedroom before I could get any feeling back into my cold limbs.

What a contrast the night hours brought. I woke before dawn, my body feeling as though it was on fire. I switched on the light and saw a terrible image peering back at me. The other side of my face had now swollen up, so my features were totally distorted. The spots were a deeper red and the bald patches showed through the tangled mass that was my hair. What a monster! I couldn't face leaving my room to eat. I called to my father that I wasn't well and would be remaining in bed. But I prayed fervently that day; oh, how I prayed to God for my health to return.

Incredibly, the following morning, the spots had gone and so had the swelling on my face. I still had the bald patches, of course, but otherwise I had received what I thought was a miracle cure. Was it the power of prayer, the water, or the blast of winter sunshine I'd received at the pond? Who could tell, but the disappearance of my facial afflictions lifted my spirits.

It was now February and I had been out of touch with David for weeks because I simply had not been able to use a phone to call him and he had no means of getting in touch with me. I certainly wasn't going to risk another taxi ride to his house. In recent weeks, no less than four women had called on my father asking if he would give permission for me to marry their sons. I will say this about him—he at least showed me the courtesy of asking me, and each time I refused. His face always showed his disappointment and I worried about how much longer he would allow my refusals to continue before he took matters into his own hands.

War was now inevitable. George W Bush was moving his navy into position. His battle commanders were talking to allied nations such as Britain and Australia, briefing the coalition of the willing. Countries were either for America or against them. Kurdistan could hardly wait for the war to start because the feeling was that this time it would be the end of Saddam Hussein. Even the local channels in our home were now carrying news about the military build up. My father seized every chance to catch the latest bulletins.

What would David be doing as the scent of war drifted across Iraq and into Kurdistan? I was desperate to talk to him but it was out of the question. Out of the question, that was, until one of my aunts Whaffa, put a proposal to my father. Seeing how unhappy I was, she suggested to him that I could work for the company where she was employed. With my father listening, she told me that the company was in need of people who could read and write English. There was an opening for someone who could convert documents and feed the data into a computer. I was more than eager to take up the job, but there was a condition. It would be an entirely voluntary position—I would not receive any pay. I nodded my head in agreement, trying not to show how overly excited I was at the prospect of being away from the house for much of the day.

Next, Whaffa had to talk to my father alone, discussing the pros and cons of the work. They were together for an hour before she came into my room; I was hired! Another of the conditions I had to adhere to was clothing. She would be responsible for choosing what I wore to work. I guessed what was coming, and I was right. She selected the most drab, colourless outfit she could find in my closet, so that when she came to collect me the following morning I was dressed in a long grey coat over a baggy kaftan. I felt no need to complain, though. This was relative freedom!

The offices of the company, which manufactured pipes and agricultural machinery in a nearby factory, were housed in a typical white-painted building in the centre of Dohuk. The boss, Ahmed Zumar, was a portly man in his 50s who greeted me warmly and described the kind of work they were involved in. He mentioned in passing that sometimes they dealt with the UN, discussing various projects for the future. My heart leaped—could it be that David might call by one day? Wishful thinking, I told myself.

I was led into what would be my office, a small, cheerless room, where a 28-year-old man who introduced himself as Diyar was crouched over a computer. He was, I was informed, the company's computer whiz and while he knew everything about the machines he wasn't able to read the English language documents that had to be typed into them. That was to be my job.

With his jet-black hair and Johnny Depp lips, which broke into a smile when we were introduced, I took an instant liking to Diyar as he began to show me the paperwork and discussed the work I would be doing.

What a relief it was going to be working with someone as personable as him. My aunt had already told me, as we drove in, what an adorable young man he was and I wondered at the time whether she was already thinking of the word that worried me so

197

much: marriage. Well, I was determined I would give this person, whoever he turned out to be, no encouragement. Now, in the office alone with him—although the door was kept ajar—I could see why she might have been thinking he was the perfect partner for me. His family, it transpired, were well off and he had the good looks that parents of brides look for.

Any fears I had, however, began to melt away as he began to tell me that his parents were trying to arrange a marriage between him and a cousin. He had been told that as he had failed to find himself a future bride, it was time one was chosen for him. They had selected a pretty girl, he said, but he just didn't want to marry her because she reminded him of his sister. The pressure, though, was increasing because they had been trying to get him wed for the past three years. So, I thought, it works that way for the men as well as the women.

Ahmed came into the office and explained that I would probably only be working for him for three weeks or so, when the pile of documents had been translated and the data fed into the computer. After that, there would be no more work for me. Nevertheless, it would be three weeks when much of each day would be spent away from that grim house where my grandmother lurked.

'I'm sure we can get it done very efficiently,' Diyar told his boss, adding with an emphatic smile towards me, 'now that we have an English genius among us!'

In following days, as he busied himself with the workings of another computer and I typed up the data, I told him a little about my life, with a few twists. I didn't want him to know all my business so I explained I had decided to come to Kurdistan to live with my father, who had decided on a patriotic return after years of living in Australia.

I could tell that the work was likely to stretch beyond the

estimated three weeks because I could only be at the office when my aunt was there. As soon as her day was over, so mine ended. It was a mirror image of my first job with Zana, from whom I had heard nothing. So much for sworn vows on the Koran. But like that first job, my presence depended on the presence of an aunty.

Much time slipped away as Diyar and I talked about my background in Australia and about his in Dohuk. He told me that in terms of life's experiences 'we Kurdish people are amateurs compared to people like you from Australia'. I assured him that was not the case, but failed to add how much I hated the culture and the way women were treated. Diyar was a great practical joker, if not a little childish. Staring from the window, he would suddenly cry out something like: 'Oh look, Michael Jackson's just arrived!' and I'd be on my feet hurrying towards him before I realised he was having me on.

Diyar's tribal background was different to my own Misseri. He was a Bamerny, from beside the Turkish border, whereas my family's tribe was from further south and was influenced more by Arab culture. Within my Misseri tribe is the Brifkani clan, who are regarded as coming from a holy land within the Kurdistan region. In fact the body of a respected holy man lies in our region and attracts many visitors who hope to receive a blessing there. Such discussions kept Diyar and I distracted and very little work was getting done, although we always made out we were busy when we heard footsteps approaching from the corridor.

Much of my work involved typing in information about village populations, the number of houses, how many water metres were connected, that kind of thing, but I needed Diyar to help me understand how to use Excel, a totally new program for me.

'Do you pray?' he asked me one day.

'Yes, five times a day.'

'You, who grew up in Australia, pray five times a day! I thought foreigners were not into religion. Let me hear you recite part of the Al-Fatihah.'

Was this a test of my honesty? Or did he just want to listen to a foreigner reciting the opening surat, which gives thanks to God of whom there is only one. I recited it and his face was a huge smile.

'And for Ramadan, did you fast?'

'Of course.' I did not tell him that no food had been available each day during that observance even if I had wanted to eat. Between the rising and the setting of the sun, it was forbidden to have anything.

'My, you are a real Kurd!' And he broke into a gleeful laugh, clapping his hands.

There came a day when I knew he would ask the inevitable question.

'Are you engaged to be married?'

He would have already known that, I suspected, from what my aunt might have told her boss, Ahmed, but I gave him the answer, anyway, that I was not and had no intention of getting married unless it was to someone I really loved. I could sense that he was 'moving in' on me, but I was determined to put up my defences, constantly aware of my 'terrible' secret. A further hint came from my aunt as we drove to the office one morning.

'What do you think of Diyar?' she asked. I told her that I thought he was very nice and had a good sense of humour.

'Well, they are all from a strong Islamic family and very well off. His father teaches the Koran in schools, you know, so Diyar is very religious. He impresses me with his devotion to God. Yes, Latifa, I agree with you—he is a very nice young man.'

If that wasn't a strong hint to encourage Diyar I didn't know what was.

At the office on that particular day Diyar was much quieter than usual, almost glum.

'What's wrong with you, Diyar? You're always so cheerful.'

He hesitated before replying. 'I have things on my mind.'

'Tell me, what things?'

'Just things. . . well, okay, I'm afraid of rejection.'

'What are you talking about?'

'Don't worry about it.' Then he walked from the office and I heard him pacing up and down in the corridor. I wondered what the other workers might have thought because they would surely have seen him. When he returned he came and stood right beside the chair where I was typing.

'I want to send my mother to your house,' he said. I couldn't prevent the intake of breath. I had suspected this was coming, but now that the words had been spoken I didn't know how to react. With anger or gentleness. Should I tell him that it was preposterous to make a marriage proposal to someone after just a few days? Or should I peacefully kill off his hopes before they were allowed to rise any further?

'Diyar,' I said. 'I've become used to mothers calling around at my house but this is the first time a man has asked me directly. I'm flattered that you've asked me. But, well, it's just too soon.'

I thought that was the easiest way of telling him no.

'I'm in love with you,' he said. 'I want your hand in marriage.'

This was too much pressure.

'I feel your energy, your presence,' he continued. 'I've never met any woman who makes me feel this way. You are the true representative of a good, holy and modest Muslim woman.'

Oh dear, I thought. If only he knew my true background. If only he could see the turmoil within.

'I want to walk through the city with you as my wife. You would make me so proud.'

'Diyar, we've known each other for just a few days. As much as I like you, I cannot even contemplate marriage. Please don't send your mother around to the house. I'm still a young woman. I'm not ready.'

'I know how old you are. You are nearly 23, so you are not young.'

'Who told you how old I am?'

'Your aunt. She has told me so much about you. Twenty-three is not young. The girls here are getting married at the age of 13 and I want to show my love to you before you get much older.'

This extraordinary conversation was taking place with the office door ajar. I wondered if our voices could be heard in the passageway. The concrete floor of the office would have bounced the sound out through the door and I asked him to speak more quietly.

'I'm not ashamed of people hearing. I love you.'

I had to keep him at bay without hurting his feelings. He had impressed me at the start of being a fun-loving young man and the last thing I wanted to do was turn him into a woeful wreck by rejecting him. It was obvious he was infatuated with me—but love?

'We have only a short time here together, Diyar, before my work will be over,' I said. 'Let's not spoil our friendship with any kind of emotional tension. I'm sure that after I leave we'll be able to continue our friendship and then, who knows. . . ? In the meantime, you must concentrate on your work. Do you want to get fired?'

'They won't get rid of me. I'm their computer whiz,' he said, and the thought of his value to the company seemed to distract him from the topic of our conversation.

That night I contemplated the latest drama that had enveloped me. How could I spend another two weeks in that office with Diyar? He would certainly not give up now that he had revealed his feelings. The following day he said nothing of our conversation and seemed to be his normal friendly self as he worked on his computer. But I was aware of his eyes on me throughout the day and occasionally he would mutter to himself, but loud enough for me to hear:

'Focus—I must focus on my work.'

Then he would jump up from his desk and walk out into the corridor where I could hear him pacing up and down. 'Focus, you must focus', I heard him telling himself. His aftershave filled the room, a scent that had not been present on the day I had started. He seemed to me even more groomed than when I had first met him. This was pressure of the highest order. I was trapped in a cell at home and now I was trapped in an office cell with this obsessed young man.

One day he brought in a box full to brim with papers and placed it on my desk. He asked me if I could have a look for a particular document and as I leafed through the papers I arrived at a small velvet box, purple in colour, with Arabic carvings around it.

'What's this?' I exclaimed, although I had a sinking feeling about what it contained.

'It's for you. Open it.'

'I can't accept a gift from you, Diyar.'

'Yes, you must.'

'Very well, but I won't open it here. I'll take it home.'

He agreed and as my aunt had to leave early that day, it meant I was home before my father and while my grandmother was out. I went straight across the road to my friends and showed them the box, which had remained unopened.

As they crowded around it, I slowly opened it. The third oldest girl, Warvin, a serious shopper when she was allowed into town with relatives, gasped. 'Oh my, he is so rich!'

We were looking at a gold ring, encrusted with rubies around the band while the centrepiece was a huge royal blue sapphire surrounded by a ring of tiny gold balls—and around them was a circle of diamonds.

'Latifa, I can tell you now that there are only three of these in the whole of Dohuk. I've seen the remaining two in the jeweller's whose name is here on the box. They call this the Angel Ring and it's from Dubai.'

I couldn't believe my ears when she told me its value—at least $US20,000.

'His family must have been keeping it for the time when his marriage will be confirmed,' said Warvin. 'Some families do that. He must have asked his parents for it. Oh, Latifa, he is very serious about you. Does it mean you are going to marry him, now you've brought the ring home?'

'No way!' I cried. 'It's going straight back in the morning. But please don't tell any of my family about this. They'll just force me to continue with this boy if they find out.'

Back in my room I twisted the ring around between my fingers. The diamonds sparkled in the overhead light. I had never handled anything so beautiful in my life. But what was a beautiful gift for a girl if her heart remained cold?

'I cannot accept this,' I told Diyar the following day, handing the box back.

His face fell. 'But I have told my family all about you. They gave it to me to pass to you. This will humiliate me and them.'

I felt terrible about hurting him, but my guilt quickly changed to defence when he suddenly lashed out. 'Do you know how many girls would love to be in this position? I have a good family, I am a caring man, I have everything that any girl could wish for. Yet when I hold my hand out to you, you reject me.'

'Diyar, please understand. Sparkling rings or money can't buy my love. I have to feel it.'

'So you don't love me?'

'I like you. You are a good man. But I cannot get married to a man I've known for a couple of weeks. I can't make a lifetime commitment just like that. Things must be allowed to develop.'

The atmosphere was tense for the remainder of the day. I breathed a sigh of relief when my aunt popped her head around the door to say it was time to go home.

Even from my bedroom I heard the gunshot. I ran out of the room to look for my grandmother and asked her if she had heard the noise. She told me to go back to my room while she checked outside. She returned to tell me that the crowds who had gathered in the street informed her that a young man had killed himself with a bullet in the head because the girl he loved had been forced to marry someone else and this was her wedding day. But the tragedy was even greater—it transpired that he had earlier gone to the girl's house and shot her. It was a big shock to me. Was love so strong that you could kill the one you loved? It had to be so—crimes of passion stretched even into the heart of Kurdistan. What worried me was my own position now with Diyar. I had rejected his ring, and I had to see him the next day.

I was full of trepidation when I returned to the office the following morning. But Diyar greeted me with his old smile. I wondered whether it was an act or if he was genuine. In any case, within an hour, he laid a small paper box, surrounded by a bow, on my desk. Oh no, I thought, here we go again.

'This time you have to keep it,' he said. 'Don't embarrass me again by giving this back to me. For the sake of God. I would still like my mother to come to your house. I will do anything to prove my love for you—anything.'

That was how he continued for the remainder of the day. The pressure was still on. But I felt obliged to take the small box home with me, knowing full well that it contained a ring. When I brought it out I could see that it was not as valuable as the other band, but it was still very beautiful, with a gold oblong-shaped centrepiece inscribed with Arabic calligraphy, the script being interspersed with tiny diamonds. I could read the words. 'There is only one God,' they said.

'In that case, God,' I thought, 'give me some direction.'

To that end when I said my evening prayers, I asked again for holy guidance. Then I lay on my bed and considered my position. I had tried to escape over the border and failed. I had been promised assistance from Zana and David and nothing had materialised. My father and his mother were keeping me as a virtual prisoner until the day I married and if and when that day came, all would be revealed about my 'personal' status. And knowing how my father had beaten me just for trying to get away, I had no doubt that he would carry out his threat to kill me next time I, in his eyes, disgraced him.

I also remembered Sheireen, the former Sydney schoolfriend I had met in Dohuk. I had run into her again in Dohuk where she had been forced into a marriage to her cousin. She said that when she and her husband returned to Australia she would do what she could to help me. What had become of her promise?

The one way out of Kurdistan for women who had relatives living abroad was to marry a man who would want to leave with her to be with those relatives. Alternatively, if the new husband had relatives the wife might be able to persuade him to take up his roots and leave Kurdistan. Marriage was the only way out for any girl trapped.

Suppose I was to agree to marry Diyar? If he was truly besotted with me, as I believed he was, he might well agree to leave for Australia with me. He had told me he would do anything, absolutely anything, for me. Once I was married, my father and his mother would have no further say in what I did. But of course there was that one outstanding problem. My virginity. Or lack of it. Our wedding night would reveal all and not only would there be uproar there would be murder. Mine.

But what if I was able to break the news to Diyar that I was not a virgin? If he accepted it, then my escape from Kurdistan was virtually assured. If things didn't work out between us once we reached Australia, it would be easy enough to get a divorce. But if he didn't accept it. . . ? I thought hard about that serious problem. And I remembered how religious he was. I believe I could take advantage of his devotion to God. I didn't like to think of such things but I was desperate and unless I did something for myself—anything—my life would be short. There would be a forced marriage and all would be revealed.

I made a decision that night before sleep carried me away to skies that were big and blue and where the ocean washed up onto my favourite beach, Bondi. When the right moment came I would tell Diyar my secret.

SIXTEEN

I just had to pick the right moment.

When I next saw Diyar I thanked him for the ring and told him that because it came with the love of God—and his love too—I would keep it. He asked if I was going to wear it, but I said I would wait until I was invited to a wedding to put it on special display. I also hoped that because girls who attended weddings were allowed to wear jewellery, it wouldn't attract attention from my father and relatives who would also be among the guests.

'But please, Diyar, no more gifts.'

'There is just one more. Tomorrow, make sure you bring a bag in with you with some papers and clothes, just general things, in it.'

I jokingly asked if he was planning to rush me away somewhere, but he was deadly serious. So the following day I arrived at the office with one of my larger handbags that had been filled with plastic bags, on top of which was a kaftan that I told my watchful grandmother was a 'spare' I wanted to keep at the office.

It was a day when Diyar shared slices of a cake he would bring in every two weeks. I set to work on the computer as he went around the building with the cake. On his return, he told me he had saved the best part, which had small pieces of fruit on it, for me. He told me to take my time eating it and when I asked why he explained that the sooner I got through the pile of documents that had to be translated and typed up, the sooner my job would be over and that was the last thing he wanted. So the cake was a delaying tactic. Clever, but it would have only gained him an extra half an hour of my time at the office. He was obviously desperately in love with me.

He asked me if I'd brought a bag as requested. When I put it on the desk, he said it was needed for this—and he propped a box, slightly larger than a shoe box, on my desk. Inside was a single rose. And a fluffy teddy bear. On the back of the bear was the word HUG.

'Where on earth did you get this, Diyar?' It was a cute gesture demonstrating again his desperation at winning my heart. He had asked a cousin in Baghdad, who had to travel to Dohuk on business, to bring the bear and the rose. He was not to know it, but the rose reminded me of St Valentine's Day in Australia, when roses would turn up on my doorstep from anonymous schoolboys, accompanied by cards declaring their love for me. The bear and the rose were the reasons for him asking me to bring a bag, so I could fit them in to take home.

I asked him why I had to be so secret about it. He said he had read my concern about his approaches and did not want my father or grandmother to see the items in case they thought I was being courted by someone and they added pressure on me to get married to him. He said he accepted I was not to be rushed, so as a sign of respect to me he thought it best that my father and grandmother should not see his gesture of love at this stage.

This incident led me to believe that I might be able to bring him so close to me that he would understand that what had happened to me in the past was the result of rape. I tested the ground, asking him what he knew about Australia. He had heard about kangaroos and the Opera House and he responded enthusiastically when I asked if he would like to go there one day. Perhaps this was it. Diyar could well be my way out, providing he could get over the virginity problem. Marriage to Diyar would be self-serving for both of us.

I had to bend the rose a little to make it fit in my bag, and over the top of it place the bear and the clothing I had brought to the office with me. My grandmother suspected nothing when I arrived home but I was sad about having to hide the rose and the bear in my closet. I unlocked the cupboard which had all of my secret items within it, such as my diary, CD player and my Tracy Chapman music and lay Diyar's gifts with them, locked the cupboard door again and placed the key back in its hiding place.

There was about a week's work to be done when I decided to tell Diyar my secret if the opportunity arose. I had devised a plan to ensure that nothing could go wrong. He had continued telling me each day how much he cared for me and how wonderful life would be together, even though we were from a different tribe. He even made a joke of him being the 'computer whiz' and me being the 'English genius'. He had now gone beyond the dream of marriage to me, asking if I had a daughter, what would I call her?

'I'm going to have grey hair if you keep yourself from me like this, Latifa,' he said. 'Please don't keep saying no. I'm not like this normally. I've never declared my love like this for any woman. You're a Muslim woman who prays five times a day, a Kurdish woman. It's not like you're a Buddhist or an Arab or Jewish. You're like me.

You are perfect for me. I will give my life for you. It is the biggest sacrifice any man could ever make.'

I believed the time had come.

'Diyar, I am not like the other Kurdish girls you have met.'

He smiled at me as he sat on his seat, just a metre away from my desk. 'I know. I know what you are going to tell me.'

I was shocked. 'You do?'

'Yes, you grew up in a Western culture. Your background is different. But that's okay, I can accept that.'

I felt tears in my eyes. He was so innocent. 'There's more to it than that.'

'Then tell me. I don't care what it is. Just tell me.'

'I don't know if I can trust you enough to tell you.'

'Oh, you can trust me, Latifa. You can trust me with anything. You should surely know that. Anything at all.'

'Diyar, I know there are girls who would be willing to throw themselves at your feet. Even though I am very fond of you, I am trying not to fall for you because I am not your perfect woman. I am not a perfect woman.'

He jumped to his feet, his eyes aflame. 'So you do have feelings for me. This is the first time I have heard you speak from your heart. I don't care if you can't cook or if your Kurdish isn't perfect. Cooking is not important. I don't care if you don't like doing the washing. And the way you speak Kurdish, with a bit of an English accent thrown in, it is so cute.'

He was at his most vulnerable. This was the moment. I stood up and he stood up. I walked to him and put my hand on his arm, the first time either of us had touched. I felt him shudder at the contact.

'What I am about to tell you must be a secret between you, me and God,' I told him. He nodded his head in agreement. 'And because it

211

must be that way, you must swear your silence on the Koran.'

His head jerked back. 'Never have I been asked to swear on the Koran,' he said. 'This must be a very important secret. But I will do it for you, Latifa, I will do it for you.'

As was the tradition, there was a Koran in the office, in its highest place, on top of the cupboard. As he placed it on my desk he told me that he did not believe it was right for anyone to use the Holy Book to protect themselves, but in my case he would make an exception.

'I understand that,' I said. 'But this is extremely important.'

With his hand on the Koran and his eyes on the ceiling he declared on the holy word and on his love of God that what I was about to tell him would remain a secret for the rest of his life.

My head was down. I felt a great shame. Then his hand brushed the hair back from my face. I still had bald patches, but I had learned how to cover them well with the rest of my hair.

'Now you can tell me,' he said.

I started to cry, wiping away the tears with my sleeve and praying that no-one would come in.

'It wasn't my fault. . . What happened wasn't my fault.'

'What—what are you talking about?'

'It was my cousin. . . He betrayed me. He. . . ' I grabbed Diyar's hand. 'Oh, dear Diyar, I am not the one for you because I am not a virgin.'

His whole body went rigid. He almost jumped back, like someone leaping from the strike of a poisonous snake.

'You slut!' he cried. 'You filthy whore! You know it is *haram* (forbidden) to speak to prostitutes like you—and you have touched me. You disgusting bitch! How dare you come here to Kurdistan with your slutty Western ways, representing your father's good name. I wash my mouth of you. Every word I have spoken to you is damned. You disgust me! You are filth!'

212

And then he spat at me, striking me in the face. I felt his venom running down my cheeks, mingling with tears that flowed out of sorrow and fear.

He returned to his desk and I could see his jowels moving as though he were grinding his teeth. The ensuing silence was too much to bear but as though on cue my aunt entered the office and told me her work was over for the day and we could leave. She noticed Diyar's stiff, white face as he glared at the computer screen and asked if he was all right—he looked unwell. Perhaps, she suggested, he had taken on too much work.

He shook his head and she took the hint to leave. I followed her out, expressing ignorance about the reasons for his appearance.

What a terrible night followed. I lay awake trying to decide which was the more powerful—Diyar's absolute hatred of me or his devotion to God. If his hatred won, I would be lost, for he would make sure my father knew what I had told him. If his love of God won, he would keep his word and remain silent. Once again, my life hung in the balance.

What added to my misery was the knowledge that there was about a week's work to be done before I could be released from the company. A week in that office with Diyar.

But a shock awaited me when I arrived the following morning. Diyar was not there. He eventually turned up an hour late, unshaven, his hair uncombed. 'There's no need for you to remain here,' he snapped. 'I have finished all our work.'

Although all the computer processing had been completed between us, there had still been a large number of documents to be put into order. He had taken all the paperwork home and spent the entire night working on it so that I could be dismissed early. Without a further word to him, not even an imploring word for him to remain silent about my secret, I picked up my bag and walked from the office.

I told my aunt, in an adjoining office, that all the work was finished and that I was ready to leave whenever she was. She asked me to wait for half an hour or so. As I sat trembling after all that had gone on between Diyar and me, I cast my eyes about my aunt's office. She had been working as a mechanical engineer, the only female in the company, for many years and was held in great respect by the men because of her strong Islamic dress sense. Despite her long employment, her office was totally soulless; just a desk, brown curtain, a simple chair and nothing on the wall but a cheap clock and a framed verse from the Koran. A simple plant or a flower in a jar would have given the place a lift, but she had lived with God and nothing of beauty for so long that she was totally satisfied with her surroundings. It was the way it was in most homes and offices in Iraq.

While I waited, I started sketching abstract designs on a piece of paper she gave me but my thoughts were elsewhere. There was now a man who hated me and who knew my secret. Not a man who loved me and cared for me, but a man who loathed me. What was my secret doing in his 'care'? What a fool I had been. But it was too late now. My fate hung in his hands and the strength of his love of God. I still had that ring he had given me. And the teddy bear. What was the point of returning them, even if I had the opportunity? I had no doubt he would have regarded them as tainted objects, touched by an unclean woman.

My work finished, it was back to the confines of my father's home and the dark face of my grandmother. A month went by before my aunt said: 'Guess who's just got married? Your friend Diyar. He's married his cousin. Isn't that wonderful news?' So he had taken her on the rebound from me. My secret was safe as far as his telling his bride about me was concerned, but there was always the danger that he might tell my father should anything at all upset him.

The US battleships were moving into the Gulf. Saddam Hussein remained defiant. The Middle East braced itself for the inevitable war, which everyone knew would break out within weeks.

My father had a surprise in store. He had beckoned me into the men's room to ask me 'about something'. Now what, I wondered. Another crisis? I was expecting to hear the name David, or Diyar on his lips, but it was Jamilla. A woman in her 40s, she was living with her younger brothers as tenants in a house my father's family owned in Mosul. My father said that the divorce from my mother, Baian, had been completed and he wanted my blessing to marry Jamilla. The big shock was not the marriage plan but the fact that he had asked for my blessing, which I readily gave. As time was to later tell, she had to dye her dark blonde hair black because it reminded my father and his family too much of my mother.

There was a reason for his marriage plan. 'I know that one day you are going to get married here and I'm going to need someone to look after me in my old age.'

These Kurdish men, I thought—all they could think of is how they could turn women into slaves and he obviously had me earmarked for the same kind of miserable life. Yet this was the first time my father and I had had a decent conversation since the beating he had given me. Jamilla, who was eight years younger than my father, had been a guest at his wedding to my teenage mother and was actually a distant relative.

Just a week after obtaining my blessing, the wedding went ahead. A small gathering at the house because my grandmother made a point of mentioning that after all the time that had passed—four years—she was still in mourning for her son. When I say 'small' it was still very colourful. The Islamic ceremony had taken place in a house where Jamilla was staying with an aunt, the event being witnessed by three male relatives, my grandmother and the following day came the celebrations. Compared to many Islamic weddings, this was a mild affair. The more valuable the bride (judged on her beauty) the more gold she receives from the husband. She could receive up to 10 kilograms of gold in jewellery and then be expected to wear it. There would be bracelets running up her arms, earrings, ankle bracelets, rings, a necklace and a gold head piece. It is amazing they can even walk! But after three or four days it is common for the husband, whose family has given the gold, to take it back to sell, and pay his debts. Only the rich girls get to keep their jewellery.

My father's bride was picked up by my father from the aunt's house where she had been staying and a beep from a ribbon-decorated vehicle outside told everyone that my father had arrived with his new bride, Jamilla, in her white gown—accompanied by one of his sisters and his mother. Women from along the street had gathered outside their homes and began calling with a 'whoop', 'whoop'—their way of expressing their delight. Jamilla was escorted into the house, women holding her gown and her arm, for this was not only a wedding celebration; it was the 'foreplay' before her official deflowering. Even so, despite the lovely gown she wore and her carefully-applied make up—the only time she'd be allowed to wear it—she still had to retire to the women's room with all the others while the men spread themselves out around the house and garden. I had put on a colourful Kurdish dress, black and silver with a silver belt and, looking at Jamilla's sad face I could tell that she was not 100 per cent happy. She had been very close to her brother, with whom she shared the rented house, and this was the parting she knew had to come or, with the years going by, she would remain a spinster. Now she was sitting in this closed-off room, saying nothing, as the other women sat talking among themselves and staring at her, as though she were a stone idol on display. I managed to speak to Jamilla, as all the women sat in one room and the men in another, as usual, about how I and my brother and sister had grown up in Australia and perhaps one day she might persuade her new husband, my father, to take her there. That, I hoped, could lead to my escape.

The men as usual had their lunch first, a meal of various meats, rice with nuts and currants, *tirshik* (a stew of meat and onions in a soup) and the famous *dulmah* (stuffed vine leaves) after which boxes of sweets were passed around. Everyone drank juices and tea, the closest to alcohol being grape juice. For me this was a wonderful occasion, for my prison home had become a place of gaiety, except for the poor bride and if only for a few hours for me. My grandmother had hired a woman to do the cooking and one of them told me her sad story, even though it had been expected of me to entertain the guests. I wanted to stay in the kitchen and listen to what she had to say. Hearing someone's story took me away from my own misery. Her husband had been executed by Saddam Hussein's secret police—she did not reveal his 'crime'—and because she was then deemed to be a single woman her children had been taken away from her and given to her husband's family because her own parents had passed away. Another woman relayed to me the hardship of each day, with her husband ill and unable to work, which meant she had to run between two cleaning jobs to support him and their six children.

When the men had devoured all they could eat, the remainder of the food was sent into the women's room, where it was laid out before the bride. She was invited to take the first mouthful and then the women joined in but I could see that Jamilla did not feel in the mood for eating.

Finally after boxes of sweets had been handed around and the children cried with tiredness, it was time for everyone to leave—including me. I would be staying at my aunty Khalida's house because this was the night when only the married couple, my grandmother, the bride's aunty and one of my father's old uncles and his wife would be allowed to remain to witness that the 'breaking in' of the bride had occurred.

I felt so sorry for Jamilla. This should have been such a personal celebration between a happily married couple whose love affair had been allowed to blossom. But of course, this was the way it was done in Kurdistan. On my return to the house the following day the men crowded around my father, congratulating him on the start of his new married life, but the bride was kept from view, it being deemed discourteous to see her after the wedding night. Discourteous after those relatives had been hanging around outside the bedroom door to wait for my father's successful appearance!

Jamilla wore a maroon Kurdish gown that day and sat once again in the women's room. The only times I saw her were the occasions when she went to the bathroom. That night, for the first time, they retired to my father's room, which he had furnished with a new bedroom set. The following day it was straight into the housework. There was to be no honeymoon. Such happy events did not exist. Jamilla coped with her new rules well, for having lived with her brother for so long she was quite used to the daily routine of washing clothes, cooking, doing the dishes and sweeping floors. There was one occasion in the first week of her marriage when one of my aunties told her to take a rest—but my grandmother, hearing those words, scowled at the suggestion. Such was the control my now 65-year-old grandmother held over this second woman in the house—me being the first, of course—that when Jamilla wanted to visit her brother in Mosul she had to virtually beg for permission. Even then she was told she could not remain for the week she had requested and had to return after three days. The time was to come that when a second request to visit her brother was made, my grandmother refused outright, leaving Jamilla in tears. I would ask her to sit with me for a short time to watch the latest news about the war threat, but she would always reply: 'No, your grandmother is on her own.'

When she did take time away from the housework—which we were both sharing—to sit with my grandmother in the women's room, I would see my grandmother hogging the heater while Jamilla was forced to sit further away, shivering. On one occasion my grandmother saw a CNN news feed on the local channel, which we were now receiving because the war was all that anyone wanted to hear about, and when she saw an American reporter she commented: 'Just look at that woman.' Then, to the woman on the screen, she said: 'Are you wearing enough make-up, you slut?'

Aware of her mother-in-law's fierceness, Jamilla went out of her way each day to please her. She must have mentioned something to my father because I heard him tell her: 'You must show her respect. She's an old woman.' Not so old to be tough, though, for she was always walking to the shops to bring back groceries and, as a former fashion designer, she was also often doing embroidery on an old pedal-operated sewing machine, calling out to Jamilla from time to time for her to do this and that. She had positioned the machine in the front window so she could see who was coming in through the gate. I wondered if the day would ever come when I would see her smile.

'You're not just married to my father,' I thought, as I saw Jamilla's daily distress. 'You're also married to my grandmother, you poor thing.'

But I was no better off, of course. At least it was officially accepted that she was no longer a virgin. My own secret hung in the balance. Would Diyar break his word and go to my father with my confession? Each morning I woke with that fear on my mind and it was only when I lay down at night did I thank God that another day had passed without a new threat to my life.

Sometimes I would ask myself how mentally strong I really was. My body had protested against my treatment as revealed in the outbreak of spots and the shedding of my hair—I still had the bald patches—but I wondered whether, in relation to other girls who might find themselves in the same position, I was being incredibly strong or behaving like a wimp.

'No, you're not a wimp, Latifa,' I told myself. 'Fight back if you must, but do not give in to this culture which will eat you alive if you succumb to it. Love God by all means, but that does not mean you must love the way of life that tells you to pray each day. If you do lose your life fighting to retain all that you believe in, well, that is how it will have to be.'

Such things I repeated frequently as the weeks passed after my father's wedding. I was shackled, that was true, but I was determined it would not be for the rest of my life. Whenever I was doing the dishes or helping Jamilla in the kitchen I would plug in my earphones and listen to Tracy Chapman, sometimes humming with it. Because I also had a tape player, I would sometimes play it softly in the kitchen when my father and my grandmother were out, but I could tell this scared Jamilla because this was Western music, which had always been so foreign to her, and she feared the worst if she was to be caught enjoying it. I had other music, including Aretha Franklin and Sade—but I couldn't play Sade without bursting into tears because it was too romantic and reminded me of David. How would I ever see him again? He had obviously found no escape for me because I was certain he would have found a way of getting the message to me, even if it was by sending a kid from up the street to call on the girls across the road to pass it on.

As I watched Jamilla's daily misery in the presence of my grandmother, I wondered if my mother had also had to endure the same pain from the same woman. My mother had been taken from her home at a young age to live with my father and his own mother—and her husband when he was still alive—and I now recalled words that she had uttered just once when we were living in Sydney: 'Your father's sisters, your aunties, are two faced and as for your grandmother, she put me through hell.'

I could imagine that, enduring the same hardships, but the thought of what my mother may have endured could not bring me to forgive her for what she had done to me. She had betrayed me and I would never, ever forget that.

SEVENTEEN

At 5.30 on the morning of March 20, 2003, allied forces began bombing Iraq. As Tomahawk missiles and GBU-27 bombs struck Baghdad, Special Forces teams from the US, Britain and Australia, which had already been covertly positioned on the outskirts of the city, hit specified targets. Ground forces began moving up from the Gulf. The war had begun. For Saddam Hussein there was no turning back.

The Kurds had been waiting for this for years and even from the first scent of war in mid 2002 had been preparing their own battle ground in the mountains bordering Iran, where fundamentalists who supported Osama bin Laden had been expected to launch an attack against the Peshmergas.

While it was obvious from the news reports that war was about to break out, there had been more than enough evidence for the Kurdish people that nothing could stop it. The Americans had been bringing supplies in from the Turkish side of the frontier, huge trucks laden down with weapons, missiles and heavy machinery that passed by on the highway near Dohuk. The word was that they would be setting up bases at strategic points in Kurdistan. But I had found out in another heartbreaking way that Iraq was soon to be in turmoil. I was shopping with my aunty in central Dohuk when, standing at the roadside, I noticed a convoy of four-wheel drive vehicles approaching. I knew what they were immediately. Blue and white flags fluttered on the bonnets and there were blue letters on the side that made my heart pound: UN. David and the UN staff were leaving!

Each of the 10 or so vehicles had tinted windows so I couldn't see into them. But they all went past me and I knew, I just knew, that David was in one of them—and he could not have failed to have seen me. Could he have wound down a window and waved? Probably not. But what hurt me was seeing him leave without warning. Again, I thought that he might have been able to get a message to me via a child. There was always a way if someone really wanted to make contact. He had clearly done nothing to help me. Just upped and left. I loved him dearly and now he was gone. But I had also betrayed his trust in me. Perhaps the stakes were even.

However, when the convoy turned a corner and vanished from sight I felt that my one and only contact with the 'outside world' had been severed. I used the edge of my scarf to dab away my tears. I did not want my aunt to see them. It was as though my heart had been ripped out. I felt empty and betrayed. David had told me he loved me, yet he had slipped away like a thief in the night.

The departure of the UN vehicles left me and the rest of the town in no doubt that war was upon us. I had also watched the daily news broadcasts to keep abreast of events, but all the signs were right outside my door. Not only my neighbours but the entire population of Dohuk were getting out of town and heading to the villages, fearing that as a last stand, Saddam Hussein would turn his wrath on the Kurds, his long-time enemy. At the mention of Australian special forces on the TV I had an immediate dream of a team of heavily armed troops rushing into town, scooping me up and carrying me far away! I certainly did not want to be caught up in a war zone after all the misery I had endured. Memories of what my mother had told me, how the Arabs had slaughtered the Kurds with their chemical bombs, flooded back to me. No wonder people were now clearing out.

When I was able to slip across the road to the girls' house, just before they packed up their bags to leave, I saw footage on Al Jazeera of the blasts in the night sky over Baghdad. Saddam Hussein's forces were putting up resistance, but it was clear the allies were routing them. Would the Arabs then turn their attention to the Kurds? Would Saddam's forces be driven north for a last stand, crushing the Kurds in their advance? Such thoughts flooded my mind.

'Dad, everyone is leaving. Aren't we going?'

'We're going nowhere. I fought for Kurdistan when I was younger and I'm not leaving my country now. This time Saddam will not defeat us.'

'But if we leave, we'll survive. Isn't that a form of winning?'

'We will survive,' he said. 'The Americans have learned from their mistakes in the Gulf War and they won't make the same mistakes again.'

'What about the chemical weapons Saddam has?'

'We don't know if he does have any. If he does, I've made preparations for you and your stepmother.' He went to his room and returned with two ancient gas masks. 'If there is a chemical attack, put these on and make sure your stepmother puts hers on.'

'But what about you and your mother?'

224

'We will remain and see it through.'

This was nonsense. Why couldn't we just leave for the relative safety of small villages like everyone else?

I stood at the gate and watched the cars go by, laden down with bags of rice, cooking pots, squawking chickens in cages. Soon, it seemed, we were the only family left in the neighbourhood. I had become so used to hearing children laughing, cars honking, but now there was just silence. All the shops were closed and boarded up. My father stretched tape on our windows to prevent the glass shattering and falling in. We were in a ghost town.

I was weighed down with despair. Bouts of dizziness hit me through the days as the bombings continued in the south and getting up each day became a struggle. It was not the fear of war coming to us. It was the feeling of being totally isolated in this house, alone with poor Jamilla, my father and his joyless mother. Despite the empty streets and the knowledge that there were no boys around to gaze at me, I was still not allowed to step outside the gates to stretch my legs, to stride out and get some real exercise. I had been so active in my schoolgirl days and now all I did was bend my knees to clean floors or stretch my arms to make my bed. Little wonder that I had put on so much weight.

My father kept the radio on day and night. He spent most of what should have been sleeping hours listening to the news but every one of those four televisions in the house was also on, picking up feeds from the major networks. Then I heard the distant pounding of bombs and feared that it was Saddam's forces turning on the Kurds, but my father assured me that it was the Americans hitting Mosul where many of Saddam's forces were dug in. Our house shuddered as each bomb hit, even though the attack was many miles away.

Then came the pictures that the whole of Kurdistan had never imagined—images of Saddam Hussein's statue being pulled down.

In no time, it seemed, those families who had fled were pouring back into Dohuk. The fall of the statue was the tangible sign to the Kurds that the tyrant had been defeated. The sound of car horns echoed through the streets, guns were fired into the air. People danced and cheered. My father gathered up his AK-49—a sophisticated version of the omnipresent AK-47—and let loose a volley of celebratory shots in the street.

'Praise be to Allah!' he cried. 'Praise be to the Americans!'

I heard my grandmother tell him: 'I wish your father was here for this day.' For my paternal grandfather, who had passed away in 1996, had, like my own father, been a Peshmerga. Like my father, though, I was told he had a temper that was easily aroused.

The Kurdistan Government organised a big party in a central park to which everyone was invited. There was a band which sang freedom songs and even dancing, while the Kurdish flag—red, white and green with an image of the sun in the middle—fluttered on a tall pole. The local TV played songs by a famous Kurdish political singer, Shivan Perwar, who came to prominence after the 1988 chemical attack. For once, there was no mention of the Koran on the local networks. The screens were filled with war news and pictures of people dancing. My father cried with happiness at footage of Peshmerga fighters shaking hands with American soldiers to the north of Dohuk. There was talk of the allies setting up a provisional authority. Saddam's reign was over, although he had disappeared.

'They'll find him and he will get his punishment,' said my father, as life began to return to some form of normality. I knew that the Americans had set up bases in the region and I thought that if I could reach them they might be able to help me, somehow, to escape back to their world, back to normality. But there was no way, of course, that I could reach them and no assurance that they would be able to help with their focus on the aftermath of the war. Beside the war was not really over. Pockets of fighting were breaking out everywhere. There was an added difficulty. If I broke away from the house and contacted the Americans and became delayed for any reason I could not bear to think what my father would do to me. I had never forgotten his threat that if I ever brought shame in any way to him again he would have no hesitation in killing me.

I lived with that threat daily because I had no way of knowing whether Diyar's hatred of me would simmer away to the point when it boiled over and he went to my father with the secret I had relayed to him. My father was often cleaning his gun and he had asked me on several occasions before the war to go fox hunting with him in the mountains. I had always declined because I simply didn't want to be alone with him when he had a weapon in his hands. It would have been easy enough for him to turn it on me in a flash of anger, for any reason.

As the Americans set up their northern bases, my grandmother and my father travelled to the telephone exchange to tell their relatives overseas that they were safe and well. My father did not call Baian and although I was allowed to go with them I was allowed only to speak to cousins that they telephoned. My mother had not bothered to send any messages inquiring about my welfare; not that I expected her to. If anything, I believed she should have arrived months earlier as the war clouds were looming to get me out of Iraq, but that never happened. How I longed to speak to my young sister, Bojeen. So often against the thunder of distant bombs did I bring out a photo of her and cry over our separation. She must have been bewildered at having had to return to Germany without me two years earlier.

The months rolled by as I continued my daily routine at the house. Mothers came and mothers were sent away with my continued refusals. My father made reference now and again about how I was not getting younger and hinted that time was running out before he would insist on my taking a husband.

Once or twice during the summer I would travel with my father, Jamilla, his mother and two or three of his sisters for a picnic in the hills. We would lay out a rug under a tree and eat our bread and meats and sip fruit juices. I breathed in the fresh air taking as much as I could into my lungs, for I did not know when the next time would come around, if ever.

Then, as the winter of 2003 began to set, he took me for a drive through the snow-capped mountain ranges, pointing out that it was in those icy conditions that he had run from the hills in his bare feet on hearing the news that I had been born. That was how my journey had begun, for the loss of his shoe with his personal information inside had resulted in the entire family fleeing from execution.

The Americans were still fighting pockets of resistance north of Baghdad as December came—and hunting for Saddam Hussein. His evil sons, Udai and Qusai, had been killed in a bomb attack in July after a tip-off about their hideout in Mosul and how the women in Kurdistan had rejoiced that these evil rapists, who threw women from helicopters, were dead. But Saddam remained at large—until 13 December when he was found hiding in a hole on a farmhouse near Tikrit. The following day Paul Bremer, the US administrator in Iraq, made that famous announcement to a crowded press conference in Baghdad: 'Ladies and gentlemen, we got him!'

There was another round of wild rejoicing throughout Kurdistan. Saddam would go on trial and there wasn't a soul who did not believe he would receive the death penalty.

Returning from the telephone exchange one day with my father, my grandmother told me that a male cousin, Vahel, who lived in Texas, was coming to Kurdistan to work as an interpreter at an American base near Dohuk. He would be posted there for a year.

Two years younger than me, I had last seen him when I was 12 when I came to Dohuk for a visit with my mother and he was still living in the city. Since then, his family had managed to emigrate and he was now a US citizen.

I was sitting at the window when, in a gap at the foot of the gate, I saw a pair of desert boots, instead of the usual black shoes that Kurds wore, and then the gate swung open and there he was, in his full US military uniform. I was first at the door to greet him. At first he wondered who I was and I had to tell him.

'My, my,' Vahel said in the Texan accent he had adopted, 'you've grown into a real woman, Latifa!' I cringed at his words, fearing my father or grandmother would hear them and think badly of me. Vahel was the first person I'd spoken to in English since I'd been with David. We didn't hug, just shook hands. As we started conversing in English, my father came forward to greet him and immediately began talking to him in Kurdish. He was not going to allow me to speak English in his house. The unit Vahel was attached to, an administrative part of the military, had taken over a large house—one of several they had commandeered—and he was very happy there; good food, good accommodation, good people to work with. How I envied him.

I said nothing to him about my problems, but I believe he read sadness behind my smile. Several days later, Vahel returned to the house with a proposition to put to my father. He had learned that a school run by Muslim converts to Catholicism was teaching children the English language and there was a position for someone who could speak good English. If my father and then I, in turn, agreed, he said he could probably arrange for me to take the job. The position had become vacant for the most astonishing reason. The majority of teachers were converts to Christianity, but this fact was not broadcast. However, the English teacher had remained a

Muslim and had been 'caught' saying her prayers during school time. The principal had told her that no Muslim prayers were allowed and she was asked to leave. I was amazed that the school had not been burned down!

To my surprise, my father agreed I could take the job. But he didn't know about the school's Christian background. He explained to his mother, 'If she's doing nothing but talking to children, then that's all right.' I would be earning $US200 a month for just four days a week from 9am to 4pm. Of course, I, too was saying my prayers daily, but I would cross that bridge when I came to it.

I was picked up by a staff member and enjoyed my first day at the school, using colours and numbers to help the children learn English. I even got the youngsters, aged from six to ten, giggling as we played musical chairs to set them at their ease with me. The other teachers commented that my class seemed to be particularly happy but asked if I was keeping the children to their lessons. I told them that learning could be fun and I noticed that they, too, began introducing games. After a couple of weeks, a play was put on by the older children in the school and it was during a break that the school principal said there was a young woman, Haveen, among the audience I might be interested in meeting. She was an Australian Kurd!

Unbelievably, she was also from Liverpool, four years younger than me. A very pretty girl, she told me a story that was not exactly new to me. Her parents had brought her to Kurdistan, retained her passport and she would not be allowed to leave for Australia until she married and took her husband with her. On her return to Sydney, though, she planned to divorce her husband.

How I enjoyed listening to her descriptions of the area that I knew so well. The Westfield shopping centre had expanded to the point I wouldn't recognise it, and there were now many Kurdish people in the Liverpool area. One vital question I had to ask her, without revealing my own situation, was: 'Are you a virgin?'

She looked at me in bewilderment. 'Of course I am—I don't want to be murdered.'

Her answer alarmed me, for it brought home once again my own perilous position.

While I enjoyed teaching the children, I found I was getting constant migraines. I believe it was a combination of my own stressful position, the general noises of the school after the relative silence I had been forced to live in and the fact that Americans were close and I had no means of trying to get to them to ask for help, even if they could to anything for me. My father, too, was asking me if I was maintaining my daily prayers at the school. I told him the truth, that praying during school hours was not allowed, which was why I wanted to quit. I told him I did not want to miss my daily prayers.

'I'm proud of you for putting Allah first, ahead of your job,' my father said. His words were a big plus for me, for it was my intention to continue to win his trust. I could hardly believe my ears—but then he read my prayer activities as another sign that I had sunk deeper into Kurdish culture and that the next step might be marriage. I believed that the closer the ragged bond grew between us, my father might become more flexible about my movements.

But there were times when he would just snap at me, a flare-up that I had no doubt was sparked by my unmarried status. Sometimes I would catch him staring at me with tight lips, his eyes slits, like a man holding back fury. I became so worried about his up and down moods that I began to take precautions for my safety at night. Fearing that he would creep into my room and smother or strangle me—as some fathers had done to their 'wayward' daughters—I stood a bowl containing some of my jewellery, on edge against the door, so it would crash down on the marble floor and wake me if he tried to creep into the room. Etab, my cousin who had been burned and shot in the desert, and I shared the same great grandfathers, so my father had his blood coursing through his veins. Honour killing was in the family. Would I be next? Always, over and over again, that question returned to me.

Depression overcame me. I couldn't face going to school. My body and mind felt as though a great weight were pressing down upon them. When the staff member called to pick me up as usual I told him I was unwell—and to pass on a message to the principal that I felt I couldn't return any more. Later that day, a teacher turned up at the house to beg me not to give up, telling me that the children were missing me but I shook my head sadly.

The following day she was back with pile of cards signed by the children, all imploring me to return. 'We love you and miss you, Aunty,' was the general message. I was deeply touched but I believed it was wrong to carry my depression into that classroom of innocent young children.

So once again I was back to my household duties, sharing them with Jamilla. It was painful going into town for the shopping with my aunties, for the Americans were everywhere, doing their own shopping when they were off duty, driving around, smoking, laughing, grinning at the women who did their best to avoid their eyes. Except me. I did my best to attract their eyes and often they would meet mine, but they had obviously been well briefed on the local custom—make a fleeting glance if you dare, but don't take it further and above all, don't touch!

Does God really answer prayers if you pray hard enough? I believe he does because I prayed every day and night that the arrival of the Americans would bring some relief to my soul-destroying daily routine. A male cousin, Vasheen, came to the house with my Texan cousin Vahel, smiled at me and told me: 'We've been talking about you, Latifa. And we might have some good news. But first we have to ask your father.'

Always my father. I was an adult, but everything depended on my father. It was several hours before my father called me in to the men's room in the absence of my cousins. There was, he said, a job going as an interpreter with the Americans, with a unit called the 416th Civil Affairs, whose job it was to liaise with local communities. He would give me permission to work with them as long as there was a woman who would be working with me and my safety could be guaranteed. He had been given those assurances by Vahel and the answer was now up to me. I had to fight back the urge to shout: 'Yes, yes, of course I'll take the job!'

Instead, aware that I must always remain in my father's good books in case anything went wrong, I replied: 'I'd love to take it, as long as I can continue with my daily prayers. They are most important to me.'

That answer pleased him and he said I could start as soon as the opening could be arranged. But he had one further message for me, which turned my heart cold.

'While we are appreciative of the Americans and what they have done in defeating Saddam Hussein, do not give them any personal information about yourself. Do not get involved in any close conversations with them. Keep your business strictly that—business. If I hear anything about you that is not appropriate, anything that displeases me, I will kill you without question.' Once more, the threat.

The following day Vasheen drove me to a large house that the unit had taken over. At the gate, we were met by another of my cousins, Riving, who was also employed by the military. He got us past the guards at the gate—where snipers looked down from command posts—and as we entered the compound, which was completed surrounded by sandbags and razor wire, I could see that it embraced not just a large villa but several other houses as well. Sandbags were piled up against the windows. These people were well prepared for any late assault by straggling members of Saddam's army or guerrillas determined to make a last stand.

I was introduced to the colonel in charge, a burly, grey-haired man in his 50s who appeared bemused at seeing a Kurdish woman without her headscarf—I had taken mine off and had adjusted my hair to hide my bald patches. He made me welcome and I felt immediately comfortable in his presence.

He began showing me around the main villa, where the offices were housed. In one office, where sandbags were again piled up at the window and where there were maps on the wall, personnel were sitting around a large desk, most of them dressed in a brown T-shirt, military issue. They said 'Hi' and raised hands as I was introduced to them. This is where I would be working for most of the time, I was told. When a lieutenant came in, he took one look at me and said: 'Whao—and who is this?' It was just wonderful to hear someone speak of me in such a warm, jocular way—in English! When he heard me speak and learned I was Australian he raised his eyes in amazement—and so did the others. It was hard for them to understand that an Australian woman, who was also a Kurd, should be 'hanging around' Kurdistan when there was a war going on. It was too difficult to start explaining to them that my presence there was against my wishes. My cousin Riving was still with me and I did not want to risk him passing anything of my conversation with the Americans back to my father.

They fired many questions at me, though. What the hell did that stuff called Vegemite really taste like? And there were the inevitable questions about kangaroos and crocodiles and sharks. I felt so homesick, but hid my sorrow.

It was arranged I would start in two days time, a Saturday, after the day of prayers. My father wanted to know few details about the actual work I would be doing but insisted on knowing who I would be working with. I put his mind at ease by lying that there were Kurdish housekeepers in the office and, as icing on the cake of my lie, I told him there was even a prayer room.

He informed me that he had arranged for a taxi driver to pick me up each morning and collect me again at the end of my day's work. The driver was a cousin called Mohammed, who was also, chillingly, the brother-in-law of the murdered Etab. I felt it wise not to question why he was chosen.

There were seven military men and one female in the military villa where I would be working. They were very accommodating and showed me around the place again, just as they had on my introductory day. I 'clicked' with the one woman, Joyce, a black American, who set about telling me all the problems she had with her husband, mainly because he was back in the US and she was in Kurdistan.

My duties were photocopying, answering the phone and typing data into a laptop. I settled in well because everyone was so friendly, but the day came when I was asked to do an interpreting job— two of the sergeants needed to speak to the mayor of Dohuk, who couldn't speak English. I was concerned about going into town with two men, but this was my job. If my father got to hear about it, I would have to bear the consequences.

We rode into town in a Humvee, or Hummer, a wide-bodied military vehicle with its add-on rooftop weaponry. When the US military moved, they took no chances. Such was the respect the Americans had among the Kurds that we were ushered straight in to see the stocky, bald-headed mayor at his office, which was adorned with photos of Mustafa Barzani, the founder of Iraqi Kurdish resistance. We sat around a glass-topped coffee table but before the discussions began I was alarmed to see a man enter with a video camera. He was from a local TV channel and the last thing I wanted was to see my picture on the evening news. My father would see the vision of me sitting among those men and I couldn't imagine the punishment that would follow. I quickly pointed out my difficulty to the mayor's assistant and he reached an agreement with the cameraman not to include me in his shots. A simple mistake like that could have cost me dearly.

I was amazed at the information I was privy to as the Americans asked questions of the mayor and I interpreted. They wanted to know how weapons came into the country from the north, which country supplied them and the routes along which they were delivered to the south. While the meeting lasted less than half an hour, I was glad to leave—it was too high-powered for my liking.

But I had pleased the Americans and word went around the compound about what they considered to be my efficiency. While I was not going to tell the colonel that I was uneasy attending the meeting I asked him if, whenever it was possible, I could remain in the presence of women. I explained my sensitive position with my father.

'No worries, mate!' he said, trying to imitate an Australian accent. 'Why didn't you say so before?'

The unit was often invited to barbecues and at first some of the men were a little worried about accepting, asking me if they thought it was safe. 'Are they likely to ambush us, or poison the food?' I was asked. I assured them that it was most unlikely and to make sure that things were safe I agreed to accompany them, along with Joyce. I couldn't help thinking that here was I travelling with a group of tough American soldiers to ensure they didn't fall into any danger!

Of course, I did not tell my father about the barbecue, which was held on the outskirts of town and the hosts were unknown to my family.

After a week or so I became friendly with one of the lieutenants, who I will call Matt. He was always asking if I was settling in and to let him know if I had any problems. I had no impression at all that he was 'chatting me up'—he was a straight, honest guy. He was a man I just knew that I could trust. One day, when I was alone in the office typing up a review of a meeting they had had, he stood beside me and said: 'What's wrong, pretty girl? I can tell something's up with you.'

'I've got things on my mind. It's nothing to do with work. It's a personal thing.'

'Hey, don't let it boil up. Let it out. Tell me what it is. Maybe I can help.'

'I'm not comfortable about talking about it.'

'Try me—what have you got to lose?'

He was right. What did I have to lose?

So I looked up into his face and told him I wasn't a virgin.

EIGHTEEN

'You've got a problem,' he said, understanding immediately. 'A real big problem.'

I didn't need to be told that, but it helped to hear that someone else appreciated it—and didn't spit in my face.

'What can I do to help?' he asked as I went on to describe my father's very real threat to kill me.

I told Matt that if there was some way of getting in touch with the Australian Embassy in Iraq, I'd be able to give them my passport details and they would be able to verify my citizenship—and do something to help me escape.

Matt told me to wait while he wandered off to another office, where there was an internet connection. He returned with a print-out of the embassy, its address, email and phone number. Of course, I knew its location because I had driven close to it with my sleazy Baghdad cousin but what I had not possessed was a phone number.

'Why don't you call them right away?' he said, nodding towards a telephone.

I couldn't believe what was happening. Was it really going to be as simple as that?

It took time to talk my way past a receptionist and I was then put through to a consular official. I told him that I was an Australian citizen of Kurdish heritage and I was trapped in Dohuk. I knew I was blurting it out and I felt Matt touch my shoulder and whisper: 'Relax.'

The official's next words stunned me. 'You have to come in to the embassy and explain this to us.'

'I can't do that!' I cried. 'Don't you understand? I'm way up here in the north. I have no money nor any means of getting to you! I would need a man to drive me to Baghdad and there's no way that any man would do this without knowing the reason for my description. I can't tell him that I want to escape. Aren't you aware of Kurdish culture?'

On hearing my response on the phone I heard Matt mutter: 'Doesn't this guy know there's a war on? You can't drive around Iraq like you're on a darn picnic.'

I asked the official to take down my old home address in Sydney and my passport details so he could verify who I was. The response I had was: 'Unless you can come in to the embassy, there's nothing we can do.'

'Please, please! Even if I could get to you, my family would know I've gone missing and they'll kill me. I wouldn't even reach you. They'd catch me on the way and that would be the end of me. Please understand. I'm an Australian and I'm begging you to help me.'

'There's nothing I can do unless you come in. Look, I'm busy and cannot continue this conversation. Try to come in.'

Then he hung up on me.

I burst into tears. Matt told me that he would relay my precarious position to his superiors, assuring me that it would be treated with the greatest confidence.

'We'll do what we can to get you out of here,' he said. But his words had little impact. After the broken promises by David and Zana, after the dismissive tone of the embassy official, I held out little hope of ever leaving Kurdistan before my secret was discovered. Matt had held out a helping hand but I held out little hope of it coming to anything.

As each day passed I went about my duties, trying to remain happy but crying inside. Joyce was a great friend and in time I revealed my position to her. She was horrified and very concerned. But she assured me that if I had placed my trust in Matt and the other officers, they wouldn't let me down. Word obviously got around, but not in a gossipy way. The officers in the unit were genuinely interested in helping me and said they were looking at ways and means of doing so. As well as Matt, I was constantly being reassured by Joyce and an officer from Texas who spent all day chewing tobacco (and spitting it into a jar which he carried around).

Three weeks after I had started with the unit, I heard my aunties talking in the kitchen. Although I was in my bedroom their voices carried over the gap at the top of the dividing wall.

'What is going on with our Australian niece?' I heard one of them say. 'She is receiving all these offers from men who have rich families and she is turning them all down. We shall have to do something.'

Then I heard my grandmother's voice. 'We were hoping to marry her off soon after she arrived. She's become too much for us to handle, sitting around in her bedroom all the time. She's become a great nuisance to us all.'

Sitting around in my bedroom! It was my grandmother who had confined me to that room when I wasn't doing the housework. And she seemed to have overlooked the fact that I was now away each day working for the Americans.

Then came a comment from my Aunty Whaffa, who had taken me to work at the firm where Diyar had so violently attacked me with his words, a comment that brought a shocking intake of breath: 'I think it's time to have her checked before we marry her off.'

Dear God, they were plotting to drag me off for a medical check. I had heard that there was a hospital in Dohuk where brides-to-be were taken at the insistence of the families of some men to ensure that they were virgins. I remembered the gorgeous Pela, the girl from Sweden who had been killed by relatives. She was 'inspected' after her death and found to have been killed needlessly. She was still a virgin. Even suspicion was enough to bring about her 'honour killing'. What a misnomer such deaths were. They were murder, as plain as that.

'Is there someone her father wants her to marry?' I heard one of the aunties say.

'Oh yes,' said another. 'He's already discussed it with me. He has his eye on Ibrahim's son, Heval.' I vaguely knew who they were talking about—my father's first cousin. But it was worse than that. Much worse. For his father was Etab's father—the man who had joined in the honour killing of his daughter. Now I recalled all the compliments my father had paid to Heval over the months, vaguely suspecting that they were meant for me, but I had tried to dismiss them, believing that this was another one of those round-about approaches that had been made for my hand.

'We will have her checked and arrange with my son for the marriage within a few months,' I heard my grandmother say. 'He wants her married before she is 25 and her birthday is at the end of the year.'

'I still don't understand why she has been refusing these wonderful men. It is a great embarrassment to us all,' said a voice, to which another responded: 'It will not be for much longer.'

'And perhaps we should do something about what she is wearing to work, or have that employment stopped altogether. Have you noticed how she is dressing? You can see her shape in those clothes.'

I could hear that Jamilla, my stepmother, was in the kitchen with them, but she said nothing in my defence. She had no authority over the other women. She was the newcomer, even though, as the wife of the owner, she was officially the 'lady of the house.'

I was now well aware that I was in a race against time—receiving help to escape from the Americans or being forced to have a medical check-up at the 'virgin hospital'. That night, I felt so sick about my precarious position that I could not face the evening meal.

The following day, red eyed from lack of sleep and tears, Matt was quick to pick up that something dramatic had happened. When I told him of the conversations I had heard he cried: 'Oh shit. It's full speed ahead for us, then.'

Matt went off and pulled strings with his superiors. It was arranged that I should be taken to the office of the Coalition Provisional Authority (CPA). The headquarters was housed in a building adjoining one of the city's big hotels and it was there I was introduced to one of the senior co-ordinators, who I will call Rob, for security reasons. A tall man in his 40s with steely grey hair, he was dressed in civvies as he held out his hand. He had already been briefed about my case, but brought out a yellow note pad and jotted down all my details—full name, passport number, background in Australia, when I left, when I arrived in Kurdistan. He also noted at my request—I wanted this to be made clear to anyone prepared to help me—that I was not a virgin. And that my father had slapped and beaten me and had threatened to kill me if I brought any shame to the family. I began to tell him through my tears about honour killings, but he interrupted. 'Yes, I'm well aware of them,' he said. 'Yours is indeed a very serious case and rest assured, we will get you out.'

'But please do it as soon as you can,' I urged. 'I know my time is getting short. They are already talking about taking me for a medical check-up and then all will be lost. I might not even make it out of the hospital.'

'I'll get onto the Australian Embassy immediately.'

When I told him of the reaction I had received previously, he shook his head in dismay. 'Hanging up on you without trying to seek a solution? That should never have happened,' he said.

The days rolled by. I tried my best to keep away from my aunties. I looked into my father's face, seeking a clue to his thoughts. He had remained silent about Heval and I wondered if that was because a wedding was being quietly arranged behind my back. I didn't even know Heval apart from his name. Each night I repeated the same prayer: 'Please God, help the Americans to help me. Help them to get me out of here.'

Then one day as I was translating a document from Arabic to English, despite my still relatively limited knowledge of Arabic, one of the officers, Daniel, said quietly: 'Start making preparations. You're getting out. Begin by putting your important belongings in a bag and bringing them in, a bit at a time so you don't raise any suspicion at home.'

I spun around. 'Do you really mean it? Am I really going to be leaving?'

He grinned. 'You betcha!'

So the next morning I sorted through my belongings in my bedroom, placing pieces of my jewellery, photos, my music and some light clothing that I could squeeze up into a shoulder bag without raising the suspicion of my watchful grandmother or the taxi-driver cousin who was still calling to collect me each morning. My hands shook with excitement as I packed in the bright red top I had owned since I was 17 and which I had been forbidden to wear in Kurdistan for it was the sign of a loose woman. I was careful not to put in too much for I knew I would have several more days to sneak things out.

The next day, I told myself, I would smuggle out more of my jewellery and my diary, which contained so many truths about my grandmother and my aunties. I didn't want to leave the diary at the military unit overnight because, even though I trusted all around me, I was still worried that it might fall into the wrong hands. So I locked it away in the closet, planning to remove it some time in the coming days. I stared at the shoes and the clothes my aunties had bought for me. They could definitely stay behind!

As my cousin drove me to the headquarters that morning, the bag with my belongings at my feet in the back seat of the taxi, I kept telling myself to remain calm—and to be prepared for another disappointment. If another let-down came, though, I knew it would be disaster for me. Time had run out.

At the office, I dropped the bag at my feet while I waited for the opportunity to ask where I could store it.

'You have your stuff? Great!' It was Daniel! 'You'll be leaving in five minutes.'

It took a second or two for his words to sink in. Then I was hit by a flash of doubt. Leaving for where? Was I being sacked? Were they going to take me home because I was, as I'd heard my aunties say so often in the past, 'too much trouble'? And why so soon, when they had told me that it would be a week or so before anything could be done? Surely, something had gone terribly wrong.

Before I could say anything, he added: 'There's a vehicle waiting for you. You're going to be taken to Mosul and from there to Baghdad and then—home, baby!'

He read the delight in my eyes and my intention, as I pushed back the chair, to throw my arms around him with thanks. He backed away slightly. 'Hey girl, don't make it too obvious! There's only a handful of us who know what's happening. Your case has been top secret—and I mean top secret.'

'Except from me,' said a new voice. It was Matt, who had come into the office, grinning. 'Back to kangaroo land for you,' he said, throwing me a wink. 'Told ya we'd be getting you out.'

Then they gave me my instructions. A very careful plan had been mapped out to ensure there were no leaks back to my father. They would be using a Kurdish driver employed by the military to take me to what I would tell him was the home of a make-believe aunty and from there I would be transferred to another vehicle. I would not be giving the driver the address, though.

'How will I know where it is, then?' I asked.

'I'll give you instructions with my finger,' said Daniel. 'When you see which way I point as we travel, you tell the driver to go that way.'

I had just enough time to hurry into an adjoining dormitory to say goodbye to another staff member, Trevor, who had been most friendly and helpful to me. I asked if it was in order for him to know I was going and was told to be quick. So I ran into the dormitory and gave Trevor a hug and a kiss and told him this was goodbye. 'I know,' he said. 'They told me a short time ago.'

We were both in tears. Then he reached into his backpack and pulled out a small package. 'You might need this. It's the best I can do.'

As we headed away from the villa in a white coloured, unmarked, four-wheel drive, I opened the gift. It was $US300, Trevor's monthly allowance for food and other expenses. He also gave me his email address. These people are just incredible, I thought, as we headed through the streets. Daniel was in the front seat and every now and then he would casually lift his hand to his face and use his thumb to indicate a right turn and a finger to indicate a left, instructions I then passed to the driver who assumed I knew exactly where I was going. I glanced back occasionally, terrified that we were being followed, but there were no suspicious vehicles behind us.

When Daniel dropped his hand quickly, it was the signal for us to stop. Then, according to my instructions, I told the driver to let me out and to take Daniel on to another military compound. I wanted to kiss Daniel's neck in thanks but of course that couldn't be done. It was just a 'thanks and see you,' kind of goodbye, with a discreet touch of my hand on his shoulder.

As the car disappeared, I found myself standing alone in the street with my own small bag and another that the military and CPA had given to me. There were houses beside me, but there was no-one in sight. What should I do? Was this a sick joke? Despite my belief in the Americans, I had been betrayed so many times that the thought came over me. I couldn't bear to imagine what my punishment would be I if was eventually brought back to my father's door by a good Samaritan Kurd who had found me wandering the streets. But suddenly I found myself surrounded by three American men, not soldiers, but armed to the teeth. They were dressed in flak jackets and had weapons in holsters on their legs and their belts. I knew who they were, having had them pointed out to me on previous trips into town with men from the unit. They were freelancers from the Blackwater security firm, a mainstay of support for the US army. They bundled me into one of three black four-wheel drivers that had driven up behind me and had parked in such a way that they blocked the street off from any vehicle that might have managed to follow me here. I recalled vaguely seeing them parked in a side street as I was driven to this spot. I was indeed at the centre of a grand escape operation.

In the car was a familiar figure. It was Rob, from the CPA. He gave me a big grin. 'You're on your way,' he said. 'Took a little bit of work, but here you are.'

As we sped from that street and began to head south, one of the Blackwater men, Ed, said: 'You're safe now. Everything's under control.'

'I just need one thing from you,' said Rob, handing me a piece of paper and a tape recorder. 'Just need you to repeat these words so we have a record that all is in order.'

It was a simple legal document declaring that I was leaving Kurdistan—and Iraq—under my own free will. What an inner thrill I had to read those words: my own free will. At last.

There were Kurdish checkpoints ahead at which police normally checked the identity of every person passing through. But because we were able to show that we were in an official US vehicle—the model was easily recognisable and Ed held out an ID as we approached—we were waved through without question. I just had to be sure I lay down flat across the back seat, with clothing over me. There would have been hell to pay if I, a Kurdish woman, was found travelling in an American military vehicle.

I was told I would be flown to Baghdad from a military compound set up at Mosul airport. The area was surrounded by razor wire and sandbags, just like the compound in Dohuk, and on the runway I could see a Hercules aircraft. I couldn't believe that this was happening. It was all so fast and unexpected. I'd left my father's home for work that morning and now I was in a US compound in Mosul, staring at an aircraft that would soon be flying me to Baghdad on my way out of this wretched place.

But it was not going to happen immediately. I was told I might have to wait for a day or two while final arrangements were made for my transportation. I was shown to a temporary building, like a trailer, which would be my quarters until everything was ready for my flight. It was fitted out with everything that I might need—including novels written in English and even a Harry Potter book! I felt as though I was already back in the West. There were snacks and a small TV and a single bed. Creature comforts indeed.

Opening the bag the men at the Dohuk base had given me, I found they had thought of everything for a girl making an emergency escape; personal medical items, a nightgown, toothbrush, toothpaste, shampoo, conditioner, comb, T-shirt, a notepad and pen, a small hand-towel, a packet of chips and a small container of juice.

Looking through these simple items I felt a great wave of love overwhelming me—their love for me and mine for them.

I dined with some of the Americans that night in the food hall, enjoying a choice of sausages, hot dogs, Asian food, fruits and all kinds of deserts. To my delight, one of the soldiers who was eating there had been based in Dohuk and we managed to have a quiet chat. He, like the others, was sad that I was leaving, but at the same time delighted for my sake. As instructed I had to pretend that I was an Iraqi journalist, but I had to make sure I kept my distance from two or three other journalists, Europeans, who were staying at the base, waiting to take the same flight to Baghdad. I might have had trouble bluffing my way past their questions about who I worked for and what stories I'd been covering and so on. Despite ensuring I stayed away from the other journalists, I was happy to be shown around the base by one of the soldiers—a move for which I was to be criticised later for showing myself when my escape was so top secret that only a few people knew about it.

As this was wartime, there were no set flight schedules. Aircraft had to come and go when it was decided everything was perfectly safe and flight paths were revealed at the last minute, so the following morning I was still told that my departure was on hold. I was uneasy about having to wait around.

A third day arrived. It was then that one of my escorts, a soldier called Donnie, said to me over breakfast:

'I don't know what that bitch has against you.'

I stared at him. 'That bitch who's in admin,' he explained, although I did not know who he was talking about. 'She's a Kurdish American but she has all the say-so around here. She's refusing to let you leave.'

He paused for a moment. Then said: 'She's insisting you be returned to your family.'

NINETEEN

I had tried to imagine what was happening back in Dohuk when I failed to return home that night. As it turned out my guesswork was very close to reality.

My cousin the taxi driver, I learned later, had arrived at the headquarters of the US Army's 416th Civil Affairs Battalion, where I had been employed, to take me home. When I did not show up, he made inquiries, only to receive shrugs. No-one knew where I was. He drove to my father's house and reported my absence. My father waited impatiently, but whether he had already pulled out that piece of cable again or reached this time for his gun to blast me down at the sight of me I don't know.

What I do know is that my planned escape placed every single American soldier in Dohuk and Mosul in grave danger. At midnight that night, following my failure to arrive home, my father, my cousin the taxi driver and an uncle turned up at the compound with weapons looking for me. The soldiers at the guard post said they knew nothing—they hadn't seen me and had no idea where I could be.

One of my relatives—and I suspect it was my father—then said: 'If any Americans were involved in her disappearance, we will turn Dohuk into another Fallujah.'

This was a reference to four months earlier when the mutilated bodies of four US contractors were dragged through the streets of the town west of Baghdad before two of them were strung from a bridge. At around the same time, five US soldiers were killed when a bomb exploded under their armoured personnel carrier. People took to the streets chanting: 'Fallujah is the graveyard of Americans.'

My father paced up and down outside the 416th compound declaring: 'If I find her, I will kill her. She is going to die this time. She will receive no mercy.' He and other family members had then toured the streets of Dohuk searching for me, pounding on doors of relatives and neighbours, their obsession at finding me driving them to ignore the time of night as they startled people in their beds.

What I had not been aware of in the lead-up to my escape from Dohuk was the official documents that had been passing between the Americans and the Australian Embassy—known then as the Australian Representative Office. The CPA, in an official report to the Australians, had outlined my predicament which had come to light in my discussions with Rob at the CPA. The official note stated that my father was in the process of arranging a marriage for me within a month. It went on to say that I had 'informed the interviewing officer that she is not a virgin and that because of her age and background it is likely she will be forced to undergo a physical examination at a local hospital as a prelude to the marriage ceremony. Whether as a result of that examination or on her wedding night, she says when it is discovered she is not a virgin, her father, whom she describes as "aggressively traditional", will kill her to save the family honour. She claims she knows of other young women who have been murdered by their families for similar reasons. This conforms to anecdotal information known to CPA Dohuk staff. . . her manner was composed but trembling. She wept briefly at several points during the interview. She appeared wholly credible and under great emotional stress.'

The report went on to say that elements of my story were believed to be true to the extent that I knew them. 'She appears to have a credible fear of physical abuse and clearly fears for her life.'

Rob had then informed the Australians that he was in detailed discussions on how best to make me 'vanish' without raising the alarm until I had, in fact, disappeared. 'The fewer moving parts and the fewer people involved, the better,' he wrote in an email.

The Australian Embassy, furnished with the vital passport details that I had written down before my mother confiscated my passport, placed my case in the hands of Stephen Rowe, the Consul General in Baghdad. This was not the same official who had hung up on me when I had called in desperation earlier. After making their own inquiries into my background, the embassy had agreed to give me consular protection and issue me with emergency travel documents. All I had to do—the same insistence as before—was to get to Baghdad. But this time I had the Americans on my side. They had agreed to fly me to the war-torn capital.

That was the plan. But then had come that potentially fatal snag. The Kurdish-American administration officer in Mosul was determined that I should not be flown to Baghdad but returned to Dohuk and back to my family—and my certain death.

Fierce arguments broke out, involving the administration officer and Rob and others who had been involved in my attempted escape, over whether I should be forced to return to Dohuk or allowed to get aboard the Hercules plane to Baghdad.

On Wednesday, 2 June, 2004—1093 days or 26,232 hours since my nightmare in Kurdistan had begun—a C-147 Hercules took off from Mosul. On board were US military personnel, some journalists and. . . me! I was on my way home!

An email from Donnie, who had been my guardian at the Mosul compound, told Rob what had happened that day.

'Just got word back from Mr Rowe that they met her on the tarmac and escorted her to their office where she was given her passport and a ticket to Down Under.'

Rob had replied: 'Whew! Now all we have to do is keep our own idiots from broadcasting the details.'

I owe my life to the Americans. They were just fantastic. They had gone out of their way, risked their lives to help me and had asked for nothing in return, not even a repayment of the cost of driving me from Dohuk, the manpower hours, the flight to Baghdad.

The Australians sent me a bill for flying me home to Sydney and for sending a representative to meet me en route in Bahrain. She was a lovely woman who gave me some women's magazines to read and asked me what I was going to do when I got back to Sydney.

'After living like a nun for the past three years,' I said, 'I'm going to go swimming naked at Bondi Beach!'

I didn't mind having to pay the bill for my fare home to Sydney. If I'd had a million dollars, I would have gladly handed it over. I wondered what the reaction would be when my grandmother and my aunties finally found the key to unlock that secret drawer in my hastily abandoned closet. My diary with my descriptions of them, my saucy underwear, a photo of David and me together and, oh yes, that raunchy movie I was looking after for the neighbours. I allowed the smile to spread across my face.

The sun was breaking as my flight touched down at Sydney

airport. I wanted to just hang around the airport, listening to the Aussie accents all around me. A friend picked me up and gave me a place to stay. My nightmare was finally over.

My mother remarried. It was no surprise to learn that her new husband was none other than my Tom Jones look-alike lawyer cousin, whom I suspected she planned to marry when she moved me and my sister and brother to Germany. As for my young sister and brother, I've lost touch with them. The ordeal which had almost cost me my life in Kurdistan had killed off my relationship with my siblings.

I've remained in touch with the Americans who helped me. Without their help I would never have made it back to the West and would probably not be alive today.

And oh, did I go swimming naked at Bondi Beach?

I certainly did—but that's another story.

EPILOGUE

I have vowed to do all that I can to help women who have found themselves forced into marriage or who live in fear of death simply because they have lost their virginity. Archaic honour killings must stop but it requires enormous international pressure on those countries where it is practised.

Even as I came towards the end of writing this, my story, I learned with sadness of two shocking cases in Pakistan.

Three teenage girls who tried to defy centuries-old traditions by announcing they intended to marry men of their choice were driven into a remote area of Baluchistan and gunned down. While they were not fatally shot, they were thrown, bleeding, into a ditch and then buried alive. Two elderly women who tried to rescue them met with the same fate.

Shortly after reports of that appalling incident reached the West came another tragic story from Pakistan. A girl forced into marriage at the age of nine to a man aged 45, went to court in the Punjabi city of Sahiwal to seek—and win—an annulment. She was now aged 17 and had spent eight years of her childhood as an enslaved wife and mother. As she left the court building she was surrounded by a group of men employed by her parents and shot dead.

It's all very well for religious groups, yes, Muslim organisations among them, to condemn these barbaric acts, but action, not words, is required.

I believe I would not be alive today to tell my story had fate not been on my side and the Americans had not helped me escape from the prison that had been my home. As an Australian, I should not have been there in the first place, but betrayal is part of a culture that believes honour is more important than the gift of life itself.

I wept when I read of the latest honour killings. There will, I have no doubt, be others. But I hope my story will help to provoke action that will chip away at ancient customs and bring freedom to all women who are forced to wear a veil, which for them is nothing more than a symbol of physical and moral slavery.